# BEI GRIN MACHT SI
# WISSEN BEZAHLT

Lukas Rieger

# Die Grundlagen des Tötungsverbotes in Peter Singers "Praktische Ethik"

**Darstellung und Kritik der zentralen Thesen zu den Auswirkungen des Personenstatus auf das ethische Tötungsverbot**

GRIN Verlag

**Bibliografische Information der Deutschen Nationalbibliothek:**

Die Deutsche Bibliothek verzeichnet diese Publikation in der Deutschen National-
bibliografie; detaillierte bibliografische Daten sind im Internet über http://dnb.d-
nb.de/ abrufbar.

**Impressum:**

Copyright © 2007 GRIN Verlag GmbH
Druck und Bindung: Books on Demand GmbH, Norderstedt Germany
ISBN: 978-3-656-31813-2

**Dieses Buch bei GRIN:**

http://www.grin.com/de/e-book/205347/die-grundlagen-des-toetungsverbotes-in-
peter-singers-praktische-ethik

**GRIN - Your knowledge has value**

Der GRIN Verlag publiziert seit 1998 wissenschaftliche Arbeiten von Studenten, Hochschullehrern und anderen Akademikern als eBook und gedrucktes Buch. Die Verlagswebsite www.grin.com ist die ideale Plattform zur Veröffentlichung von Hausarbeiten, Abschlussarbeiten, wissenschaftlichen Aufsätzen, Dissertationen und Fachbüchern.

**Besuchen Sie uns im Internet:**

http://www.grin.com/

http://www.facebook.com/grincom

http://www.twitter.com/grin_com

# Die Grundlagen des Tötungsverbotes
# in Peter Singers „Praktische Ethik"

*Darstellung und Kritik der zentralen Thesen zu den Auswirkungen des*
*Personenstatus auf das ethische Tötungsverbot*

## Hausarbeit

im Rahmen des EPG- und Proseminars „Einführung in die philosophische Ethik"

im Fachbereich Philosophie

**vorgelegt von:**     Lukas Rieger

**Fertiggestellt am:**     05.04.2007

# Inhaltsverzeichnis

# 1 Einleitung

Innerhalb der letzten 40 Jahre ist in der westlichen Welt eine Debatte darüber entbrannt, in welchen Fällen passive und aktive Sterbehilfe, also die Tötung eines Menschen, gerechtfertigt sein kann. Im Zuge dieser Debatte ist unter anderen die radikale Position, die Peter Singer in seinem in Deutschland im Jahre 1984 erschienenen und im Jahre 1993 überarbeiteten Werk „Praktische Ethik" zu dieser Frage vertritt, diskutiert worden. In nicht vielen Auseinandersetzungen ist Singer vorgeworfen worden, er leiste die nachträgliche ethische Legitimation für die vom nationalsozialistischen Regime unter dem Deckmantel der „Euthanasie", also des „schönen Todes", durchgeführte Ermordung von Menschen, deren Leben als „lebensunwert" eingestuft worden war. Er hat sich den Zorn vieler Menschen deshalb zugezogen, weil er zur Beantwortung der Frage, wann Euthanasie erlaubt sein soll, den Wert verschiedener Lebewesen miteinander vergleicht und Menschen mit schwerer geistiger Behinderung, Wachkomapatienten und Säuglingen das Recht auf Leben abspricht. Weil dieses Urteil an den Grundfesten der moralischen Überzeugungen im westlichen Kulturkreis rüttelt, ist die Diskussion oft hitzig und nicht immer sachlich geführt worden. Zahlreiche Podiumsveranstaltungen, zu denen Singer eingeladen worden war, um seine Position zu referieren, sind massiv gestört oder wegen der Ankündigung von Protesten schon im Voraus abgesagt worden. Das ist deshalb schade, weil so viele Möglichkeiten vergeben worden sind, fundiert und sachlich und deshalb überzeugend Gegenposition zu beziehen.

In der vorliegenden Arbeit soll dargestellt und kritisch überprüft werden, auf welchem Weg und mit welchen Mitteln Peter Singer wertende Unterscheidungen zwischen verschiedenen Lebewesen macht. Dabei war der Anspruch, der der vorliegenden Arbeit ursprünglich zugrunde lag, der, eine räumlich ausgewogene Darstellung der singerschen Positionen zum Verbot und der Erlaubnis Tötung menschlicher Wesen zu leisten. Im Entstehungsprozess dieser Hausarbeit hat sich jedoch gezeigt, dass sich die Kritik, die gegen das von Singer vorgestellte Modell zur Bewertung des Lebens verschiedener Wesen vorgebracht werden kann, vornehmlich an seiner Beantwortung der Frage, welche Wesen von einem Tötungsverbot überhaupt geschützt sind, festmacht. Deshalb konzentriert sich diese Arbeit auf eine ausführliche Darstellung und Prüfung seiner Thesen zum Tötungsverbot.

# 2  Zwei Modelle zur Unterscheidung des Wertes verschiedener Lebewesen

Um die Frage, warum Töten unrecht ist, beantworten zu können, muss erst geklärt werden, von der Tötung welcher Lebewesen eigentlich die Rede ist und wie man den Wert verschiedener Lebewesen ethisch relevant unterscheiden kann.

## 2.1  Die Unterscheidung Mensch – Tier

Im westlichen Moralkodex ist es unumstritten, dass die Tötung eines Menschen mehr wiegt, als die Tötung eines Tieres. Die Trennlinie zur ethisch relevanten Unterscheidung verschiedener Lebewesen läuft hier bislang also zwischen Menschen und Tieren. Ist die Unterscheidung in diese Kategorien auch gerechtfertigt?

Singer stellt fest, dass der Gedanke, der dieser Unterscheidung zu Grunde liegt, dem jüdisch-christlichen Kontext entlehnt ist[1]. Die Lehre von der „Heiligkeit menschlichen Lebens" war jahrhundertelang ein unumstößliches Dogma. Im Zeitalter der Aufklärung dürften jedoch Annahmen, die der Religion entstammen, nicht zur Begründung dessen, was gut oder schlecht sei, herangezogen werden. Deshalb sei zu prüfen, ob die Unterscheidung zwischen Mensch und Tier auch ohne religiösen Hintergrund Bestand habe.

Dazu ist festzustellen, dass die Unterscheidung zwischen Mensch und Tier eine Unterscheidung nach Spezieszugehörigkeit ist. Diese Spezieszugehörigkeit ist eine biologische Tatsache. Nach Singer ist sie aber kein hinreichendes Mittel, um ethisch relevante Unterschiede zwischen verschiedenen Lebewesen zu machen. Vielmehr bewege man sich strukturell nah am Rassismus, wenn man Ungleichbehandlungen mit dem beliebigen und in dieser Hinsicht ganz irrelevanten Merkmal der Zugehörigkeit zu einer Rasse oder einer Spezies rechtfertigen wolle. Die Ansicht, die Zugehörigkeit zur Gruppe der Homo Sapiens rechtfertige die Annahme eines besonderen Wertes ihrer Mitglieder, sei speziezistisch und nicht haltbar[2].

## 2.2  Die Unterscheidung nach dem Grad des Bewusstseins

Lebewesen lassen sich laut Singer nach dem Grad des Bewusstseins in zwei verschiedene Gruppen teilen. Die eine Gruppe ist die der Lebewesen ohne Bewusstsein,

---

1   Singer, S. 122
2   Singer, S. 122, ff.

die andere Gruppe ist die der Lebewesen mit Bewusstsein. In die erste Gruppe fallen etwa Pflanzen und Einzeller, in die zweite Gruppe Tiere und Menschen.

Innerhalb der zweiten Gruppe lässt sich weiter differenzieren zwischen nur bewussten Lebewesen und solchen Lebewesen, die Selbstbewusstsein besitzen. Bewusste Lebewesen sind nur empfindungsfähig, selbstbewusste Lebewesen sind außerdem in der Lage, sich selbst als in der Zeit existierend zu denken[3]. In die Gruppe der bewussten Lebewesen fällt etwa die Maus oder der Fisch, in die Gruppe der selbstbewussten Lebewesen fällt etwa ein gesunder, voll entwickelter Mensch oder ein ausgewachsener Gorilla. Selbstbewusste Lebensformen nennt Singer „Personen"[4].

### 2.2.1 Die ethische Relevanz des unterschiedlichen Grades des Bewusstseins in utilitaristischen Systemen

Auch wenn es einsichtig ist, dass verschiedene Lebewesen in verschiedenem Maße über Bewusstsein verfügen, ergibt sich daraus noch keine ethische Relevanz dieses Merkmals. Im Folgenden soll dargestellt werden, welche Argumente Singer für eine solche Relevanz anführt.

#### 2.2.1.1 Die Relevanz unterschiedlicher Bewusstseinsgrade im klassisch-hedonistischen Utilitarismus

Zunächst prüft Singer, inwiefern der Personenstatus eines Lebewesens aus Sicht des klassisch-hedonistischen Utilitarismus Einfluss auf das Tötungsverbot hat und ob sich aus diesem Status hier eine besondere Wertung ergibt.

Der klassisch-hedonistische Utilitarismus, als deren Begründer Jeremy Bentham gilt und der heute radikal kaum noch vertreten wird, geht von einer anthropologischen Bestimmung aus: der Mensch strebe zur Lust hin und von der Unlust weg. Deshalb sei alles, was Lust erzeuge, gut, hingegen alles, was Unlust erzeuge, schlecht. Besser sei die Tat, die mehr Lust erzeuge als eine andere Tat und schlechter sei die Tat, die mehr Unlust erzeuge als eine andere. Verursacht eine Handlung gleichzeitig Lust und Unlust bei einer oder mehreren Lebewesen, muss abgewogen und gerechnet werden: ist die Summe der Lust aller von der Handlung betroffenen Wesen größer als die Summe der Unlust aller von der Handlung betroffenen Wesen, ist die Handlung gut – im

---

3  Singer, S. 123
4  Singer, S. 119, f.

umgekehrten Falle ist sie schlecht. Das Empfinden von Lust heißt Glück, das Empfinden von Unlust Leid.

Hier fällt auf, dass der Utilitarismus auf jede metaphysische Bestimmung dessen, was moralisch gut ist, verzichtet. Die einzige Grundlage, auf der sich die ganze Ethik des hedonistischen Utilitarismus aufbaut, ist die des zumindest vorgeblich empirisch gewonnenen Menschenbildes. Eine graduelle Unterscheidung zwischen „Person" und „Nicht-Person" kennt der klassische Utilitarismus nicht, weil er mit seinen Wertungsmaßstäben „Lust" und „Unlust" nicht auf verschiedene Grade von Bewusstsein, sondern auf grundsätzliche Empfindungsfähigkeit abstellt. Dass das klassisch-utilitaristische System bei Anwendung des Personen-/Nicht-Personen-Begriffes trotzdem in der Lage ist, für beide Gruppen unterschiedliche Ergebnisse zu produzieren, soll zeigen, dass auch der klassische Utilitarismus die von Singer angenommene Unterscheidung stützt und dass deshalb personalem Leben ein vorrangiger Schutz zukommen darf.

Wie die Frage des Tötungsverbotes von Lebewesen im klassisch-hedonistischen Utilitarismus zu beantworten ist, hängt von der innerhalb des klassischen Utilitarismus gewählten Betrachtungsweise ab. Die utilitaristische Methode lässt sich mit Singer in eine intuitive und in eine kritische Richtung teilen[5]. Das, was Singer als „intuitives" Vorgehen bezeichnet, wird in der philosophischen Lehre üblicherweise „Regelutilitarismus" genannt: beurteilt wird nicht die konkrete Einzelhandlung, sondern eine Fallgruppe, unter die die Einzelhandlung subsumiert werden kann. Die so gewonnene Regel wird auf alle anderen Einzelhandlungen, die sich unter die entsprechende Fallgruppe subsumieren lassen ohne neuerliche Prüfung angewendet. Das in der Terminologie von Singer als „kritisch" bezeichnete Vorgehen wird üblicherweise auch „Handlungsutilitarismus" genannt und meint die ausschließliche Bewertung der Einzelhandlung, ohne auf Fallgruppen abzustellen.

### 2.2.1.1.1 Die „kritische" Bewertung: der Handlungsutilitarismus

Im System des Handlungsutilitarismus fällt es auf den ersten Blick schwer, ein Tötungsverbot speziell von Personen zu begründen. Im Sinne des hedonistischen Kalküls kann die Tötung jedes Lebewesens, also auch einer Person, durchaus gut sein, wenn aus dieser Tötung in der Gesamtschau der von der Tötungshandlung Betroffenen

---

5  Singer, S. 126

eine Glückssteigerung folgt. Dem Tod des Diktators etwa steht die neugewonnene Freiheit des von ihm unterdrückten Volkes gegenüber. Und wenn aus einer Tötung gar kein Glück, aber auch kein Leid entsteht, weil die Tötung völlig schmerzfrei erfolgt, besteht aus handlungsutilitaristischer Sicht nur dann ein Grund für eine moralische Verurteilung, wenn die Prognose für das Leben des Getöteten eine positive Glücksbilanz aufweist, das heißt, wenn das getötete Lebewesen in der ihm im Falle des Weiterlebens noch bis zum natürlichen Tode verbleibenden Lebenszeit mehr Glück als Leid erfahren hätte[6].

Nach Singer ist aber auch hier, in dieser Variante des klassisch-hedonistischen Utilitarismus, das personale, nicht zwingend menschliche Merkmal der Selbstreflexion Grund für ein (im Vergleich zur Wertung in präferenzutilitaristischen Systemen nur indirektes, aber immerhin personenspezifisches) Tötungsverbot: weil eine Person in der Lage ist, sich selbst mit anderen Personen und deren Situation zu vergleichen, weil eine Person an die eigene Vergänglichkeit denken und dabei Leid empfinden kann, wird die offene Tötung eines ihr vergleichbaren Wesens sie an ihr eigenes Lebensende erinnern und ihr, der beobachtenden Person – nicht dem Opfer der Tötungshandlung - so Leid zufügen. Weil es diese Leidzufügung, zumal in die Breite all der Personen, die von einer Tötung erfahren können, gedacht, aber zu vermeiden gilt, gilt es auch, die Tötung von Personen entweder zu vermeiden oder so zu bewerkstelligen, dass keine andere Person davon erfährt.[7]

In der Praxis sei die kritische Bewertung jedoch wenig brauchbar. Der Kalkül, der für jede Handlung erstellt werden soll, müsse eine Vielzahl von Einflüssen berücksichtigen, die zu erfassen, zumal in Situationen, in denen schnell gehandelt werden muss, nahezu unmöglich sei.[8]

### 2.2.1.1.2 Die „intuitive" Bewertung: der Regelutilitarismus

Die intuitive Bewertung hingegen umgeht dieses praktische Problem, weil die Entscheidungen nicht für jede Handlung neu, sondern für einige bekannte und ethisch relevante Fallgruppen schon im Voraus gefällt wird. Die konkrete Situation muss dann nicht mehr ganz neu bewertet werden, sondern nur korrekt in eine der Fallgruppen subsumiert werden und nach der jeweils gültigen Regel gehandhabt werden.

---

6  Singer, S. 137
7  Singer, S. 124, ff.
8  Singer, S. 126, f.

Dementsprechend gelange bei Prüfung der Regel „Personen sollen nicht getötet werden" auch der Regelutilitarismus unter Anwendung des oben beschriebenen personalen Arguments zu einem Tötungsverbot speziell von Personen[9], das hier aber unbedingt und generell gilt. Die (Sonder-)Fälle nämlich, in denen die Tötung einer Person von Dritten unbemerkt organisiert werden könnte, werden von der Regel miterfasst[10].

So unproblematisch und einfach in der Anwendung, wie es auf den ersten Blick scheinen mag, ist das Ergebnis des Regelutilitarismus aber keineswegs. Die Ergebnisse, zu denen man im Regelutilitarismus gelangt, hängen nämlich stark von der speziellen Subsumierung einer bestimmten Handlung unter eine bestimmte Fallgruppe und also auch mit der Bildung dieser Fallgruppe zusammen. Das eigentliche Problem, das sich dabei und im Regelutilitarismus grundsätzlich stellt, ist die Tatsache, dass der Regelutilitarismus keine genauen Anweisungen darüber gibt, wie allgemein eine Fallgruppe mindestens sein muss und wie speziell sie gerade noch sein darf. Deshalb ist beispielsweise auch die Bildung und Überprüfung der Regel „Personen dürfen nicht getötet werden, es sei denn, es ist sichergestellt, dass kein Dritter von dieser Tötung erfährt." im Regelutilitarismus denkbar. Die Bejahung dieser Regel nach Prüfung hat aus regelutilitaristischer Sicht zwar generelle Geltung, das sich daraus ergebende Tötungsverbot ist dann aber kein generelles, weil schon die Regel eine Ausnahme vorsieht.

### 2.2.1.2 Zwischenergebnis

Der klassisch-hedonistische Utilitarismus komme zu einem zwar nur indirekt wirkenden, aber doch speziell Personen betreffenden Tötungsverbot. Das sei ein Hinweis darauf, dass die Unterscheidung zwischen Personen und Nicht-Personen ethische Relevanz besitzt.

### 2.2.2   Das personale Merkmal im Präferenz-Utilitarismus

Der Präferenz-Utilitarismus ist eine Weiterentwicklung des klassisch-hedonistischen Utilitarismus. Der Unterschied zwischen beiden Systemen liegt darin, dass zur Bewertung einer Handlung nicht allein auf die dadurch beförderte Lust oder Unlust abgestellt wird, sondern vornehmlich auf die Tendenz zur Beförderung von Präferenzen. Nach Singer und dem präferenz-utilitaristischen Prinzip sind ethisch schlecht jene

---

9  Singer, S. 128
10 ebd.

Handlungen, die bestimmte Präferenzen eines ethischen Subjekts durchkreuzen; ethisch gut sind jene Handlungen, die die Verwirklichung bestimmter Präferenzen fördern oder ihnen wenigstens nicht im Wege stehen[11].

### 2.2.2.1 Die Auswirkungen des personalen Merkmals auf Präferenzen

Unter „Präferenz" versteht Singer die Wünsche und Interessen, die ein Lebewesen haben kann[12]. Die Präferenzen aller Lebewesen verdienen im Präferenz-Utilitarismus Respektierung. Dennoch lasse sich aus dem Personenstatus eines Lebewesens ein besonderer Wert dieses Lebewesens ableiten. Der Unterschied zwischen selbstbewussten und nur bewusst-empfindungsfähigen Lebewesen liege nämlich darin, dass die Präferenzen solcher Lebewesen, die selbstbewusst an die eigene Zukunft denken können, auch stark in diese Zukunft orientiert seien[13]. Die Präferenzen nur bewusster Lebewesen bezögen sich hingegen größtenteils auf ganz aktuelle Zustände[14].

Die Tötung einer Nicht-Person bedeute keine Durchkreuzung von zukunftsorientierten Präferenzen. Weil der Fisch keine Pläne und Wünsche bezüglich des nächsten Tages, ja nur der nächsten Stunde oder Sekunde ihres Lebens haben kann, sei deshalb die Tötung dieses Fisches aus präferenz-utilitaristischer Sicht weniger schwerwiegend, als die Tötung einer Person. Die Tatsache, dass sich der Fisch am Angelhaken winde sei zwar Ausdruck des Schmerzes, den der Fisch in diesem Moment empfinde, aber kein Hinweis darauf, dass der Fisch sich seines nahenden Todes bewusst sei. Gerade weil sich der Fisch aber seines nahenden Todes unbewusst sei, habe er auch keine Präferenz, weiterzuleben[15]. Die Tötung des Fisches sei deshalb im präferenz-utilitaristischen Sinne nicht verboten. Lediglich die Tötungsart, von der der Fisch durch sein Verhalten klar macht, dass sie ihn in einen Zustand versetzt, der sich nicht mit seiner Präferenz, keinen Schmerz zu empfinden deckt, sei zu vermeiden[16].

Die Tötung einer Person hingegen bedeute, ihre Präferenz des Weiterlebens (sofern nicht Lebensmüdigkeit oder andere Umstände dazu geführt haben, dass eine solche Präferenz in der Person nicht vorhanden ist) zu konterkarieren[17]. Mit der Präferenz des Weiterlebens verbinden sich auch alle anderen Präferenzen der Person, die sie bezüglich

---

11 Singer, S. 128, f.
12 das ergibt sich aus dem Gesagten in: Singer, S. 128, f.
13 Singer, S. 129
14 Singer, S. 123
15 Singer, S. 129
16 ebd.
17 Singer, S. 128, f.

ihrer Zukunft gefasst hat und deren Verwirklichung nun unmöglich gemacht worden ist[18]. Deshalb wiegt die Tötung einer Person mehr, als nur ihre eine beispielhafte Präferenz, Wohlstand anzuhäufen, zu konterkarieren. Dementsprechend ist die Präferenz des Weiterlebens schwerer aufzuwiegen als eine andere Einzelpräferenz. Die Tötung einer Person ist also die Durchkreuzung einer Vielzahl von zukunftsorientierten Präferenzen[19] und insofern schwerwiegender als die Tötung einer Nicht-Person ohne zukunftsorientierte Präferenzen[20].

### 2.2.2.2 Zwischenergebnis

Im Modell des Präferenz-Utilitarismus spielt es für den Wert eines Lebewesens eine entscheidende Rolle, ob es sich dabei um nur bewusstes Leben oder um eine Person handelt. Unter diesem Blickwinkel scheint die ethische Unterscheidung zwischen Personen und Nicht-Personen, also eine Unterscheidung von Lebewesen nach dem Grad ihres Bewusstseins, gerechtfertigt. Je höher der Grad des Bewusstseins eines Lebewesens, desto wertvoller ist sein Leben, desto mehr Schutz verdient es. Trotzdem leistet der präferenz-utilitaristische Ansatz, genauso wenig wie der Ansatz des klassisch-hedonistischen Utilitarismus, nicht die Begründung für ein generelles Verbot der Tötung von selbstbewussten, geschweige denn bewussten Wesen. Eine Handlung, die eine Präferenz durchkreuzt, ist nur dann schlecht, wenn sie nicht gerechtfertigt ist, das heißt, wenn nicht entgegenstehende, zahlenmäßig überwiegende Präferenzen die Durchkreuzung der einen Präferenz gebieten[21].

## 2.3    Das Recht auf Leben

Im Folgenden geht Singer auf den Einwand ein, dass der utilitaristische Ansatz zur Legitimierung von Verbot oder Erlaubnis der Tötung von Lebewesen auf Grundlage ihrer Empfindungsfähigkeit oder ihrer Begabung, zukunftsorientierte Präferenzen zu fassen, deshalb falsch sei, weil es ein von diesen Eigenschaften unabhängiges Recht auf Leben gebe. Dieser Einwand sei falsch, weil es einsichtig sei, dass sich das Recht auf etwas vom Wunsch oder Interesse an etwas ableite[22]. Um das plausibel zu machen, bedient sich Singer der Argumentation des zeitgenössischen Philosophen Michael

---

18  Singer, S. 129
19  ebd.
20  ebd.
21  Singer, S. 128
22  Singer, S. 130, f.

Tooley, der in seinen Arbeiten „Abortion and Infanticide" 1972 und 1983 zwei leicht unterschiedliche Modelle vorgelegt hat.

## 2.3.1   Wunsch und Recht

Das erste Modell von Tooley soll den grundsätzlichen Zusammenhang von Rechten und der Voraussetzung einer kognitiven Fähigkeit, die Tooley die Fähigkeit zum Wunsch nennt, klar machen. Die Argumentation von Tooley stellt sich wie folgt dar:

Die Verletzung eines Rechts sei nach einer grundlegenden Empfindung gleichbedeutend mit der Durchkreuzung des entsprechenden Wunsches eines Individuums. Hat ein Individuum keinen Wunsch, kann dieser auch nicht durchkreuzt werden. Dementsprechend könne dann auch kein Recht verletzt werden[23]. Also bestehe kein Recht an X, wenn kein auf X gerichteter Wunsch bestehe.

Plastisch dargestellt heißt das dann: Der Besitzer eines Autos, der den Wunsch hat, dieses Auto zu fahren, hat ein Recht darauf, dieses Auto zu fahren. Entzöge man dem Autobesitzer die Möglichkeit, das Auto zu fahren, handelte man rechtswidrig. Der Besitzer eines Autos, der nicht den Wunsch hat, dieses Auto zu fahren, habe auch kein Recht am Auto. Entzöge man ihm dann die Möglichkeit, das Auto zu fahren, handelte man auch nicht rechtswidrig.[24]

Das Recht auf Leben sei nach diesem Argument also abhängig von einem bestehenden Wunsch, am Leben zu sein. Den Wunsch, am Leben zu sein, könnten aber nur solche Lebewesen haben, die in der Lage seien, einen Begriff von sich selbst als distinkte Entitäten, also Selbstbewusstsein zu haben.[25]

## 2.3.2   Interesse und Recht

Im Weiteren stellt Singer Tooleys Verfeinerung dieses Modelles dar. Ausschlaggebend für das Recht auf Leben sei, dass das Leben zu irgend einem Zeitpunkt schon einmal im Interesse des Lebewesens gelegen habe[26]. Diese Modifizierung ist insofern eine wichtige Verfeinerung des Modells, weil sie weniger verlangt, als einen Wunsch zu hegen oder ein Interesse zu haben. So umgeht dieses Modell das Problem, das sich bei der Bewertung des Lebensrechts schlafender oder solcher Lebewesen, die nur im Moment

---

23 Singer, S. 130, f.
24 ebd.
25 Singer, S. 131
26 Singer, S. 133

nicht bei Bewusstsein sind und deshalb weder einen aktuellen Wunsch noch ein aktuelles Interesse hegen, geschweige denn artikulieren können, ergibt[27]. Nach Tooleys neuer Formulierung haben auch solche Lebewesen ein Recht auf Leben und verlieren dasselbe auch nicht durch eine Änderung ihres geistigen Zustands[28].

Das Modell vom Recht aus Interesse ließe sich laut Singer zwar auf Schlafende und Bewusstlose, nicht aber auf Säuglinge oder von Geburt an geistig schwer behinderte Menschen anwenden[29]. Die Annahme nämlich, es liege im Interesse des Neugeborenen, weiterzuleben und zum voll ausgebildeten Menschen heranzuwachsen, sei deshalb falsch, weil sie sich auf eine Ansicht stütze, die nur rückblickend, von der Warte des schon personalen Menschen aus, funktioniere. Während der personale Erwachsene rückblickend nachvollziehen könne, dass das Stadium des Neugeborenen ein für die Entwicklung hin zur Person notwendigerweise wohlbehalten zu durchlaufender Zwischenschritt sei, sei die umgekehrte Fähigkeit, vorausschauend begreifen zu können, dass dem Status des nur empfindungsfähigen Säuglings der selbstbewusste Status der Person folge und dass diese Entwicklung voraussetze, unbeschadet weiterzuleben, beim Säugling nicht gegeben[30]. Interesse setze aber wenigstens die Fähigkeit der Vorstellung desjenigen, woran Interesse bestehen soll, voraus[31]. Der Säugling hat weder einen Begriff noch eine Vorstellung davon, was es hieße, als Lebewesen in der Zeit zu existieren[32] und deshalb könne auch nicht behauptet werden, es läge im Interesse des Säuglings, weiterzuleben, um einen Status zu erreichen, von dem er noch gar nichts wissen kann[33].

Nach dem Modell von Tooley, dessen sich Singer zur Darstellung der wechselseitigen Beziehung zwischen Rechten einerseits und Wünschen und Interessen andererseits bedient, haben also Embryonen, Föten, Säuglinge und von Geburt an geistig schwer behinderte Menschen kein Recht auf Leben; Lebewesen, die sich zu irgend einem Zeitpunkt ihres Lebens als distinkte Entitäten zu sehen in der Lage waren – also Lebewesen, die in der singerschen Terminologie zu einem Zeitpunkt ihres Lebens „Personen" genannt werden konnten – haben ein solches, allerdings bloß abgeleitetes, Recht auf Leben und verlieren es auch nicht, selbst wenn sie ihren Personenstatus dauerhaft verlieren.

---

27 Singer, S. 133, f.
28 ebd.
29 Singer, S. 132, f.
30 ebd.
31 ebd.
32 ebd.
33 ebd.

## 2.4    Die Respektierung der Autonomie

Das vierte Argument, das Singer anführt, um zu zeigen, wie sich der Grad des Bewusstseins eines Lebewesens auf den Wert seines Lebens auswirkt, ist das der Respektierung der Autonomie eines Lebewesens. Autonomie sei die Fähigkeit, Entscheidungen zu treffen[34], das heißt, in einer konkreten Situation zwischen wenigstens zwei in Frage kommenden Möglichkeiten eine selbstbestimmte Wahl treffen zu können. Für die Thematik des Tötungsverbotes ist dabei die Fähigkeit ausschlaggebend, sich für oder gegen das eigene Leben, also gegen oder für den eigenen Tod entscheiden zu können[35].

Für die Fähigkeit zur Entscheidung zwischen diesen beiden Polen sei die grundlegende Voraussetzung, eine Vorstellung vom künftigen eigenen Leben und eigenen Tod zu haben. Sind einem Lebewesen schon diese Vorstellungen nicht zugänglich, stehen ihm auch keine Wahlmöglichkeiten offen. Ein Lebewesen, das keine Vorstellung von Leben und Tod hat, ist deshalb nicht autonom[36]. Die Voraussetzung zur Entscheidung und damit die Voraussetzung zur Autonomie haben also nur solche Lebewesen, die selbstbewusst sind und in der singerschen Terminologie „Personen" genannt werden. Auch Autonomie ist also eine Eigenschaft, die Personen von anderen, nur bewussten Lebewesen zu trennen in der Lage ist. Ob diese Eigenschaft aber auch eine ethische Relevanz besitzt, aus der allein sich eine Ungleichbehandlung verschiedener Lebewesen rechtfertigen lässt, prüft Singer im Weiteren.

Freilich gilt die Autonomie und damit auch ihre Respektierung in einigen, darunter den idealistischen, philosophischen Moralbegründungsansätzen als eigener Wert[37]. Dem Utilitarismus, der als eigene Werte nur Lust und Unlust, bzw. Präferenzen anerkennt, ist eine einfache, selbstverständliche Anerkennung jedoch nicht möglich. So ist Singers einziger Ratschlag, um das wertvolle Prinzip der Autonomie ins utilitaristische System zu retten, der, den im Sinne der Praktikabilität ohnehin vorzuziehenden intuitiven utilitaristischen Ansatz zu verfolgen und davon auszugehen, dass die Einziehung des Prinzips der Respektierung von Autonomie in der Regel bessere Ergebnisse erzielen wird, als ihre Nicht-Respektierung[38]. So könne auch im Utilitarismus die sich aus dem personalen Merkmal eines Lebewesens schöpfende Autonomie Ausschlag für seinen besonderen Wert geben.

---

34 Singer, S. 134
35 ebd.
36 ebd.
37 Singer, S. 135
38 ebd.

## 2.5    Bewusstes Leben

Der Entwurf, der Singers Modell von der „Heiligkeit personalen Lebens" entgegensteht, ist der, der bewusstes Leben als einen besonderen Wert achten will. Die Auseinandersetzung mit diesem Entwurf ist für Singer deshalb wichtig, weil es sich dabei um einen Ansatz handelt, der genau wie Singers Modell weder auf religiösen Grundlagen beruht, noch sich dem Vorwurf des Speziezismus aussetzen muss.

Die Befürworter des Modells vom schützenswerten Wert bewussten Lebens können dem präferenz-utilitaristischen Modell entgegenhalten, bewusstes Leben sei empfindungsfähig und also, auch wenn Selbstbewusstsein fehle, in der Lage, Lust und Unlust zu spüren. Das künftige Glück, das ein Wesen in den kommenden Stunden seines Lebens zu empfinden in der Lage ist, könnte dann aus utilitaristischer Sicht ein Argument für das Verbot der Tötung von bewussten Lebewesen sein[39]. Dieses Argument funktioniere aber nur bei einer positiven Glücksbilanz für das Lebewesen. Sei damit zu rechnen, dass das Leid, das ein Lebewesen künftig empfinden wird, das Glück, das es noch empfinden wird, überwiegt, gebe es aus utilitaristischer Sicht keinen Grund mehr, dieses Lebewesen am Leben zu lassen. So gelange man aus utilitaristischer Sicht für bewusste Lebewesen nur zu einem Verbot der Tötung von lustvollem Leben[40].

Der utilitaristische Ansatz ist aber ein universaler: er ist nicht darauf aus, die Lust eines einzelnen Lebewesens zu steigern, sondern das empfundene Glück in der ganzen Welt zu steigern[41]. Aus der besonderen Achtung des Lebens empfindungsfähiger Wesen ergeben sich deshalb Folgekonsequenzen für das ganze ethische System. Welche Konsequenzen das seien, hänge davon ab, welchen von zwei denkbaren Wegen man zur Glücksmaximierung in der Welt verfolge. Entweder wolle man dieses Ziel dadurch erreichen, das Leben der jetzt existierenden Lebewesen möglichst lustvoll zu gestalten[42], oder man versuche, das Glück in der Welt dadurch zu steigern, indem man neues Leben schaffe, das nach allen Prognosen ein glückliches, lustvolles Leben sein könnte[43]. Die erste Methode nennt Singer die „Vorherige-Existenz"-Ansicht[44], die zweite nennt er „Totalansicht"[45], weil nach ihr die bloße Summe der Lust in der Welt gezählt wird, unabhängig davon, auf wie viele Lebewesen sich diese Lust verteilt.

---

39  Singer, S. 136, f.
40  Singer, S. 137
41  Singer, S. 137, f.
42  Singer, S. 138
43  ebd.
44  Singer, S. 140
45  Singer, S. 139

Die Konsequenz aus der moralischen Legitimierung des Schutzes bewussten Lebens über die Totalansicht sei, dass man dann auch Eltern, die Kinder, die vermutlich glücklich sein würden, nicht zeugen, obwohl der Kalkül von Lust und Unlust, die die Eltern durch die Geburt ihres Kindes erführen, ausgeglichen wäre, moralisch verurteilen müsse. Dieses moralische Urteil werde aber wohl von den wenigsten geteilt. Wolle man dieses Urteil vermeiden, müsse man aber mit der „Vorherige-Existenz"-Ansicht argumentieren.[46]

Die „Vorherige-Existenz"-Ansicht nimmt an, dass es keinen Wert habe, die Summe der Lust in der Welt durch die Zeugung neuer Lebewesen, die vermutlich glücklich sein werden, zu mehren[47]. Wenn aber die potentielle Lust, die ein Lebewesen empfinden könne, kein Grund für die moralische Pflicht sei, ein solches Wesen zum Leben zu bringen, könne auch der potentielle Schmerz, den ein Lebewesen empfinden könnte, kein Grund dafür sein, es nicht zum Leben zu bringen[48]. Das decke sich aber nicht mit der mehrheitlichen moralischen Ansicht, dass es unrecht sei, wenn ein Paar ein Kind zeuge, von dem schon vor dem Zeugungsakt klar ist, dass es, etwa durch genetische Disposition, zu einem kurzen und qualvollen Leben verdammt ist[49]. Insofern gelange man sowohl bei Anwendung der Totalansicht, als auch bei Anwendung der „Vorherige-Existenz"-Ansicht zu moralischen Wertungen, die sich nicht mit der mehrheitlichen moralischen Wertung deckten.

Insgesamt geht Singer davon aus, dass nur bewusstes Leben ersetzbar sei. Stellt man nämlich zur Rechtfertigung des Verbotes der Tötung von bewussten Lebewesen auf deren Empfindungsfähigkeit und mit dem klassisch-utilitaristischen Modell also auf das Ziel der Glücksmaximierung in der Welt, könne kein Zweifel darüber bestehen, dass die Ersetzung eines nur empfindungsfähigen Lebewesens A durch ein anderes empfindungsfähiges Lebewesen B, das mindestens ebenso viel Aussicht auf ein lustvolles Leben habe, wie Lebewesen A, nur dann als moralisch verwerflich einzustufen sei, wenn die Glückssumme, die durch B in die Welt komme, durch eine durch die Tötung von A verursachte höhere Leidsumme bei irgendwelchen anderen Lebewesen, bewussten oder selbstbewussten, überboten würde.[50]

---

46 Singer, S. 140
47 ebd.
48 ebd.
49 ebd.
50 Singer, S. 160, ff.

### 2.5.1 Der Wert bewussten Lebens im Vergleich zu selbstbewusstem Leben

Nachdem Singer eingeräumt hat, dass bewusstes Leben in seinem System einen Wert haben kann, prüft er, ob der Wert bewussten Lebens auch gleich hoch sein kann, wie der selbstbewussten Lebens. Dabei macht er sich zunächst auf die Suche nach einer der Beantwortung dieser Frage angemessenen Methode. Die zu wählende Methode dürfe nicht vom Blickwinkel eines voll entwickelten, gesunden Menschen aus urteilen, denn sonst könne das Ergebnis speziezistisch verzerrt werden[51]. Es sei deshalb eine objektive Bewertungsposition vorzuziehen. Diese objektive Position könne man dann erreichen, wenn man sich vorstelle, die Fähigkeit zu besitzen, die Gestalt und Geist beliebig zu wechseln. Dann sei es möglich, im einen Moment Mensch zu sein und erfahren zu können, was es im geistigen Sinne heißt, Mensch zu sein, und im anderen Moment etwa eine Maus zu sein, und dann nicht etwa als Mensch in Mäusegestalt, sondern ganz aus der Perspektive der Maus zu erfahren, was es hieße, Maus zu sein. In einem dritten Schritt könne dann eine Position eingenommen werden, in der man weder Mensch noch Maus, noch sonst ein vergleichbares Tier sei und in der man sich deshalb mit keiner der beiden Perspektiven gemein mache, wenn man eine von beiden vorzöge[52].

Wie würde ein solch objektiver, oder wenigstens intersubjektiver Beobachter urteilen? Vielleicht würde er erfahren haben, dass die Freude, die eine Maus empfindet, diese Maus sehr glücklich macht. Vielleicht würde er erfahren haben, dass die Maus, die von ihrem eigenen Tod nichts weiß, viel glücklicher ist, als der Mensch, in den er sich verwandelt hat. Vergleiche er aber aus der objektiven Position die Perspektive der Maus mit der Perspektive des Menschen, käme er dahin, einzugestehen, dass der Schatz der möglichen Erfahrungen und damit auch des erfahrbaren Glückes beim Menschen um den schieren Kosmos geistiger Freuden größer ist, als der der Maus. Während die Maus sich nur dessen erfreuen kann, was ihr ihre Sinne darbieten, steht dem Menschen neben den Freuden, die sich ihm sinnlich erschließen, auch die Welt der geistigen Befriedigung offen. Unter diesem Aspekt, so Singer, lasse sich wohl festhalten, dass ein qualitativer Unterschied zwischen bewusstem und personalem Leben bestehe. Dieser Unterschied dürfe und solle sich auch in dem Wert, der einem solchen Leben zugemessen wird, niederschlagen. Deshalb sei es, auch wenn man nicht auf das Merkmal des Bewusstseins, sondern auf das Merkmal erfahrbarer Lust und Unlust

---

51 Singer, S. 142
52 Singer, S. 144

abstelle, schwerwiegender, eine Person zu töten, als ein bewusstes Lebewesen zu töten.[53]

## 2.6   Ergebnis

Die Richtung, in die die von Singer angeführten Argumenten für ein Tötungsverbot weisen, ist deutlich: moralisches Kriterium, um Gruppen von Lebewesen zu unterscheiden, ist der Grad des Bewusstseins, über das sie verfügen können . Der Personenstatus eines Lebewesens legt nahe, seinem Leben einen besonderen Schutz zukommen zu lassen, das heißt, seine Tötung als schwerwiegender zu werten, als die Tötung einer Nicht-Person.

Die Konsequenzen, die sich aus den Argumenten, jedes für sich betrachtet, ergeben, sind jedoch unterschiedlich. Während die Argumente über den Status von Rechten und die Respektierung der Autonomie auf ein generelles Verbot der Tötung von solchen Lebewesen, die Rechte, bzw. Autonomie für sich beanspruchen können hinweisen, ergibt sich aus dem präferenz-utilitaristischen und dem kritischen klassisch-utilitaristischen Ansatz ein nur bedingtes Verbot. Der Präferenz-Utilitarismus räumt ein, dass die Präferenz einer Person, weiterzuleben, von entgegenstehenden Präferenzen aufgewogen werden können, der kritische klassische Utilitarismus kann ein Verbot der Tötung überhaupt nur dann für gerechtfertigt halten, wenn durch die Tötung einer Person eine Gefahr für das Glück anderer Personen entsteht. Insofern ist es eindeutiger, im Zusammenhang mit den rein utilitaristischen Ansätzen von einem durch sie begründeten Tötungsvorbehalt zu sprechen.

Bewusstes Leben wird im Singerschen Konzept direkt nur über das klassisch utilitaristische Argument und nur bei einer zu erwartenden positiven Glücksbilanz geschützt. Ein indirekter Schutz für bewusstes, aber nicht selbstbewusstes Leben findet statt über den Schmerz, den der Tod eines bewussten Lebewesens einer Person zufügen würde. Besteht ein solch indirekter Schutz nicht, ist bewusstes Leben ersetzbar. Wenn aber schon das Tötungsverbot für Personen als bedingt gelten muss, so steht das Tötungsverbot für bewusstes Leben im singerschen Konzept erst recht auf tönernen Füßen.

---

53 Singer, S. 144, ff.

# 3    Kritik

Im Folgenden sollen einige Einwände formuliert werden, die sich gegen die Grundlagen richten, auf die Singer sein Tötungsverbot von bewussten und selbstbewussten Lebewesen stellt.

## 3.1    Das indirekte Tötungsverbot für Personen im klassischen Utilitarismus und die Reichweite menschlicher Empathie

Singer behauptet, aus dem Personenstatus eines Lebewesens ergebe sich im klassischen Utilitarismus ein indirektes Tötungsverbot, das speziell gegen Personen wirke. Das ist eines der tragenden Argumente für die ethisch relevante Unterscheidung des Wertes verschiedener Lebewesen. Weil eine Person fähig sei, an die eigene Vergänglichkeit zu denken und weil sie deshalb bei der Tötung an die eigene Vergänglichkeit und die Gefahr, selbst getötet zu werden, erinnert werde, sei im Interesse der Leidvermeidung von der (zumindest öffentlichen) Tötung von Personen abzusehen.

Es ist aber sehr fraglich, ob Personen ein solches Gefühl von Leid und eine solche Angst vor der eigenen Tötung nur beim Ansehen der Tötung einer anderen Person erleben. Es darf behauptet werden, dass die meisten menschlichen Personen sich, auch bei Kenntnis der singerschen Definition von „Person", eher als Menschen, als als spezielle Person verstehen. Auch der Protest, der durch die Öffentlichkeit geht, wenn die Nachricht von der Tötung einer menschlichen Nicht-Person, etwa eines Säuglings, bekannt wird, lehrt, dass sich die Empathie, die Personen empfinden können, nicht nur auf Menschen, die den gleichen Bewusstseinsgrad wie sie selbst aufweisen, erstreckt, sondern auch auf solche Menschen, die keine Personen sind. Weil aber Personen sich nicht als Personen, sondern als Menschen begreifen, kann sich das indirekte Tötungsverbot im klassischen Utilitarismus nicht nur auf Personen, sondern muss sich auf Menschen beziehen. Damit gibt zwar der Personenstatus von Lebewesen den Anlass für ein indirektes Tötungsverbot; dieses sich so ergebende Tötungsverbot ist aber keines, das sich speziell auf Personen, sondern auf Menschen beziehen muss. Insofern ist es falsch, dass sich aus Anwendung des Personenbegriffes auf den klassischen Utilitarismus eine Wertung ergibt, die personales Leben stärker schützt, als generell menschliches Leben.

## 3.2    Zum „Wert" einer Person

Singers Modell vom besonderen Status der Person ist ein Entwurf, den er explizit gegen das jüdisch-christliche Modell von der „Heiligkeit des Lebens" oder von der „Heiligkeit menschlichen Lebens" positioniert. Gerade in der Gegenüberstellung der Ergebnisse des Modells von Singer und der Ergebnisse der Heiligkeitskonzeption zeigt sich bei Singer ein großes Defizit: sein Modell kann keinen eigenen Wert bestimmter Lebewesen begründen. All seine Untersuchungen zum „besonderen Wert" bestimmter Lebewesen laufen darauf hinaus, nur vergleichende, nie absolut geltende Werte zu begründen. Das liegt an der seinen Untersuchungen zugrunde liegenden präferenz-utilitaristischen Konzeption. Die präferenz-utilitaristische Konzeption kennt als einzigen eigenen Wert die Maximierung gesamtgesellschaftlicher, idealerweise universeller Präferenzen. Dass die Präferenzen einer Person zu respektieren sind, heißt deshalb nicht, dass diese einen absoluten, unantastbaren Wert darstellen, sondern nur, dass die Präferenz einer Person in der Schau aller Präferenzen aller Personen als eine Stelle unter vielen *zählt*. Das bestehende Interesse einer Person kann jedoch durch andere entgegenstehende und zahlenmäßig überwiegende Interessen aufgewogen werden. Deshalb sind im Singerschen Konzept weder Person noch ihr Leben heilig und unantastbar. Der Person selbst und ihrem Leben kommen an sich kein besonderer Wert zu. Der besondere Wert gehört im Präferenz-Utilitarismus dem gesellschaftlichen Gesamtinteresse, an dem eine Person mit ihrem eigenen Interesse teilhaben kann.

Es ist schwer vorstellbar, wie eine solche moralische Konzeption in der Praxis wirken soll. Damit ein ethisches System in der Gesellschaft wirken kann, ist es erforderlich, dass die Gesellschaft die dem System zugrunde liegenden Annahmen kennt und sie mehrheitlich zu tragen bereit ist. Auf das Modell von Singer übertragen heißt das, dass der Einzelne akzeptieren müsste, dass sein eigenes Leben nichts wert ist, weil jederzeit Erwägungen, die im gesamtgesellschaftlichen Interesse angestellt werden, zu dem Schluss kommen könnten, dass seine Präferenz des Weiterlebens von den Präferenzen anderer Subjekte aufgewogen werden und dass es deshalb ethisch gut sei, wenn er sterbe. Das Leben in einer solchen Gesellschaft ist aber sicherlich eines, das nicht glücklich ist, sondern eines, in dem die ständige Angst vor dem eigenen Tod regiert. Es ist in diesem Zusammenhang also auch völlig unerheblich, ob die Tötung von Personen, deren Tod dem allgemeinen Interesse dient, offen oder verborgen stattfindet, weil nämlich schon die Kenntnis der der Gesellschaft zugrunde liegenden Konzeption die Kenntnis der Bedrohung des eigenen Lebens beinhaltet.

Singer könnte entgegnen, um eben solche Wertungen zu vermeiden, habe er in sein Konzept die Respektierung der Autonomie aufgenommen. Die Respektierung der Autonomie sehe vor, dass der Wille autonomer Lebewesen, also auch der Wille, zu leben, respektiert werden müsse, zu einem eben beschrieben Szenario könne es deshalb nicht kommen. Wenn aber die ganze praktische Tauglichkeit des präferenz-utilitaristischen Systems von der Einbeziehung eines utilitarismus-fremden, idealistischen Prinzips abhängt, dann ist das ein starker Hinweis darauf, dass das utilitaristische Konzept für sich nicht in der Lage ist, ein für die Praxis taugliches ethisches System zu begründen.

### 3.3 Zum „Rechte"-Modell

An der eigentlichen Wertlosigkeit des Lebens auch personaler Lebewesen in Singers utilitaristischem System macht sich auch ein weiterer wichtiger Einspruch fest. Um utilitaristische Ethik, egal ob in der klassischen oder der Präferenz-Variante, wie sie von Singer vertreten wird, überhaupt betreiben zu können, muss nämlich jedes natürliche Recht auf Leben, das sich aus bloßer Existenz begründet, geleugnet werden. Deshalb ist auch die Behauptung, ein Recht könne bloß aus einem Wunsch oder einem Interesse an etwas abgeleitet werden, im singerschen Argumentationsgang viel zentraler, als von ihm zugegeben wird. Die Vorführung des Modells von Tooley liest sich bei Singer so, als solle anhand dieses Modells nur noch eingängiger und nachvollziehbarer gemacht werden, was schon vorher bewiesen worden sei, nämlich, dass die alleinigen Bewertungskriterien zur Feststellung des Wertes eines Lebewesens dessen Präferenzen seien. Die Argumentation, die er dabei für die Entstehung eines Rechtes anführt, ist aber gleichzeitig eine Argumentation gegen die Entstehung von Rechten auf einem anderen Wege und damit gegen die Existenz von Rechten, die einem Wunsch oder Interesse vorausgehen. Deshalb ist das Argument über die Entstehung von Rechten vielleicht das zentralste Argument im ganzen Werk. Dabei ist das Modell, das er mit Tooley vorbringt, durch und durch unplausibel.

### 3.3.1 Recht und Wunsch

Tooley behauptet, die Durchkreuzung eines Rechtes sei gleichbedeutend mit der Durchkreuzung eines Wunsches. Deshalb sei die Existenz eines Rechtes auch abhängig von einem entsprechenden Wunsch. Er zeigt das am Beispiel des Autobesitzer. Es sei dann unrecht, ihm das Auto zu nehmen, wenn beim Autobesitzer der Wunsch besteht, das Auto zu fahren. Erst aus dem Wunsch des Autobesitzers, das Auto zu fahren, leite sich deshalb sein Recht am Auto ab. Dieses Beispiel und das sich daraus ergebende Resultat für den Status von Rechten ist falsch.

Der Wunsch, ein Auto zu fahren, begründet kein Recht auf ein Auto. Den Wunsch auf etwas zu durchkreuzen ist nur dann unrecht, wenn dadurch ein dem Wunsch vorausgehendes, und deshalb vom Wunsch ganz und gar unabhängiges Recht besteht, weil erst ein bestehendes Recht an X den Wunsch, X zu benutzen, überhaupt legitimiert. Hätte der A also keine Rechtsposition inne, die ihm die Nutzung des Autos sicherte, wäre auch die Durchkreuzung des Wunsches, das Auto zu fahren, nicht unrecht. Nur weil das Subjekt A die Rechtsposition des Besitzes am Auto hält, er also eine Rechtsposition schon inne hat, ist die Durchkreuzung dieses Wunsches unrecht. Hat A nicht den Wunsch, das Auto zu fahren, erlischt damit auch nicht sein Recht am Auto.

Deshalb ist auch das Recht auf Leben nicht abhängig vom Wunsch, zu leben. Das Recht auf Leben geht diesem Wunsch voraus.

## 3.3.2  Recht und Interesse

Tooleys Modifikation seines Rechtsbegründungsansatzes sieht vor, dass Rechte davon abhängen, ob das betreffende Rechtsgut zu irgend einem Zeitpunkt schon einmal im Interesse desjenigen Subjekts gelegen habe, das ein Anspruch auf das betreffende Recht haben soll. Aus dieser Formulierung leite sich ab, dass ungeborenem Leben und Säuglingen kein Recht auf Leben zustehe, weil, so Singer, das Interesse an etwas die Vorstellung vom Objekt des Interesses voraussetze. Föten, Embryos und Säuglinge seien aber nicht in der Lage, eine Vorstellung von ihrem künftigen Zustand zu haben, geschweige denn einen Begriff von Leben und Tod zu haben. Deshalb liege das Leben nicht in deren Interesse. Diese Ansicht darf jedoch bezweifelt werden.

In diesem Zusammenhang ist die spezielle Formulierung, Leben habe zu irgend einem Zeitpunkt schon einmal im Interesse des betreffenden Lebewesens liegen müssen, deshalb von Belang, weil sie, anders als die Formulierung, ein Lebewesen hätte zu irgend einem Zeitpunkt schon einmal ein Interesse am Leben haben müssen, beim fraglichen Lebewesen keine zwingende rationale Aktivität oder (Selbst-)Bewusstsein voraussetzt. Während die hier an zweiter Stelle genannte Formulierung das Lebewesen als aktiv Handelnden oder Interessefassenden voraussetzt, kommt dem Lebewesen in der ersten hier genannten Formulierung eine nur passive Rolle zu. Insofern verlangt diese Formulierung kein aktives Interesse-Fassen seitens des Lebewesens, dessen Lebensrecht diskutiert werden soll, sondern lediglich die Bewertung aus objektiver Warte, dass etwas im Interesse eines (möglicherweise geistig völlig passiven) Lebewesens liege. Aus dieser wohl bewusst passivisch gewählten Formulierung nachträglich das Erfordernis der Aktivität im Sinne einer Vorstellungs-Fassung beim Lebewesen zu fordern, erscheint unbotmäßig. Es ist perfide, zu urteilen, als Erwachsener erkenne man zwar, dass das eigene Säuglingsdasein ein notwendiger Zwischenschritt zum jetzigen Dasein gewesen sei, weil aber der Säugling diesen Zusammenhang noch nicht begreifen könne, könne das unbeschadete Aufwachsen auch nicht in seinem Interesse liegen. Aus der eigenen, geistig erhabenen Position mit der Schau auf die zurückliegende eigene Entwicklung und der menschlichen Fähigkeit zur Empathie kann dem Säugling an seiner statt durchaus ein Lebensinteresse zugeschrieben werden.

## 3.4 Die Unvereinbarkeit der Konsequenzen aus der Wertschätzung bewussten Lebens mit der ethischen Praxis

An der Stelle, an der er sich mit dem Verbot der Tötung bewussten Lebens auseinander setzt, stellt Singer zwei unterschiedliche Ansätze zur Begründung dieses Verbotes dar: die Totalansicht und die „Vorherige-Existenz"-Ansicht. Beide Begründungsansätze seien vertretbar. Es sei aber zu bedenken, dass sich aus der Annahme eines besonderen Wertes bewussten Lebens zwingend moralische Wertungen ergäben – entweder unter Anwendung der Totalansicht die Pflicht, glückliche Kinder zu zeugen oder aber, bei Anwendung der „Vorherige-Existenz"-Ansicht, nicht die Pflicht, schwerkranke und leidende Kinder nicht zu zeugen – die mit der mehrheitlichen intuitiven Wertung nur schwer vereinbar seien.

Dass Singer an dieser Stelle auf mehrheitliche moralische Wertungen eingeht, die sich offenbar mit keinem der vom Utilitarismus angebotenen Möglichkeiten zur Legitimierung des Verbotes der Tötung von bewusstem, lustvollem Leben decken, ist aus zwei Gründen verwunderlich. Erstens spricht die Tatsache, dass er dem Mehrheitsvotum überhaupt eine Stimme gibt, gegen seine Argumentation gegen schon mehrheitlich herrschende moralische Überzeugungen. Zweitens wird beim Anhören der Mehrheit, die einerseits wohl durchaus für den Schutz bewussten Lebens eintritt, andererseits mit keiner der sich im Utilitarismus daraus ergebenden Folgekonsequenzen einverstanden wäre, deutlich, dass der Utilitarismus nicht in der Lage ist, ein moralisches System aufzubauen, das mehrheitlich getragen werden kann. Ein moralisches System, das in der Praxis wirken soll, kann aber nur dann funktionieren, wenn ein überwältigender Teil jener, die innerhalb dieses Systems agieren sollen, die sich aus diesem System ergebenden Konsequenzen zu tragen bereit sind. Was Singer deshalb mit der Vorführung seiner zwei Modelle zeigt, ist vor allem eines: die praktische Untauglichkeit des utilitaristischen Systems.

# Literaturverzeichnis

Singer, Peter:  Praktische Ethik. 2., revidierte und erweiterte Auflage.
Reclam Stuttgart 1994

# Th
# Cotswold Way

## National Trail Companion

supported by

1st edition published April 2007
© Cotswold Way National Trail Office / Natural England
ISBN 978-0-9555422-0-6
Edited by Jo Ronald and Linda Cherry
All photographs © Natural England. Photographers:
Jo Ward, front cover, inside back cover and images on pages 12, 14, 16, 18, 20, 28, 34, 37, 42, 45, 54, 67, 76, 81.
Nick Turner, back cover and images on pages 2, 4, 6, 7, 8, 9, 10, 16.

**Published by** Cotswold Way National Trail Office
The Malthouse   Standish   Stonehouse   Gloucestershire   GL10 3DL
**Tel** 01453 827004
**Fax** 01453 827057
**Email** cotsway@gloucestershire.gov.uk
**Website** www.nationaltrail.co.uk
**Produced by** Cliffehanger Ltd. www.cliffehanger.co.uk

# Contents

# Introduction

The Cotswold Way National Trail follows the Cotswold escarpment for 102 miles (164km), from the market town of Chipping Campden in the north to the World Heritage City of Bath in the south. Along the way you will experience stunning views, charming villages, and experience a landscape steeped in history and rich in wildlife. The map below shows the Trail is divided into 15 easy to walk sections.

Map of the
Cotswold Way National Trail

# Introduction

This guide gives you all the information you need to help you plan an enjoyable walk on the Cotswold Way National Trail. It contains information on accommodation, refreshments, shops, cash points, public transport connections, car parking, public toilets, how far it is from one place to another and lots of other useful information.

This companion guide is not a route guide, and for detailed information about the Trail itself **The Cotswold Way National Trail Guide** by Anthony Burton is available from most bookshops or can be purchased on line (for details see p15).

The Cotswold Way, launched as a National Trail in 2007 follows the limestone escarpment on the western edge of the Cotswolds for 102 miles (164 km) from the market town of Chipping Campden in the north, to Bath in the south. The Trail predominantly follows public footpaths and although it does have some sections that follow bridleways, byways and quiet roads these sections are fragmented and the Trail is only promoted for walkers. The Ordnance Survey maps will show the sections where different classes of user are permitted (see p15)

The Cotswolds was designated as an Area of Outstanding Natural Beauty (AONB) in 1966 and was extended to become England's largest AONB in 1990.

# Introduction

Your journey will take you through quintessentially English countryside, rich in history, yet very much a living, working landscape. The walk offers a variety of scenery for you to enjoy – limestone grasslands, Cotswold stone villages, grazing pastures with dry stone walls, majestic beech woodlands, quiet valleys and stunning views over the Severn Vale to the Malverns, Forest of Dean and Wales.

Walking along the Trail is an ideal way to explore this beautiful part of the country and enjoy the local hospitality away from the bustle of the crowds. Many people walk the Cotswold Way National Trail as one continuous journey, (taking between 5 and 8 days to complete) but it can also be enjoyed in shorter sections over a long weekend or just for a few hours. Getting to the Trail is easy as it has good access by public transport. There is comprehensive, regularly updated information available specifically for the Cotswold Way (see p 12).

With the support of Natural England, the Cotswold Way is managed to the highest standards by the relevant Highway Authorites and a small dedicated team of National Trail staff and volunteers.

# History

The Cotswold landscape we see today is very much man made, yet the way the local limestone has been used for building cottages, stone walls, manors and churches over the centuries to the present day, blending them unobtrusively into the surrounding landscape, gives the area a sense of timelessness,

There is evidence of settlement in the Cotswolds dating back many centuries and examples of this can be found along the Trail. The long barrows at Belas Knap and Nympsfield on the Trail are burial chambers dating from the Neolithic period (c4,000 to c2,000 BC).

Following the Neolithic period came the Bronze Age (c2,000 to c800 BC), with the introduction of metals into everyday life. Burial sites from this period (known as "round barrows") can be found near North Stoke and in the woods at Randwick, but you will need to search for these. Further examples exist as below ground remains. These are recorded on the local Sites and Monument Records which are held by the local authorities (see p19).

During the early Iron Age (between c800 – c100 BC) people built hillforts on the escarpment, and when walking the Trail you will see why they chose these locations – the views are clear and uninterrupted, so no-one uninvited would be able to approach without being seen from a good distance away. The Iron Age settlers designed their hillforts with ditches and ramparts, and many good examples can be seen on the Trail – Beckbury Camp, Cleeve Hill, Crickley Hill and Kimsbury Camp on Painswick Beacon to name but a few.

# History

Roman influence in the area (c50BC – c410AD) can be seen from the Trail where it crosses the Ermin Way (the Roman road from Gloucester to Silchester) at Birdlip, passes close to the remains of the Roman Villa at Great Witcombe and the Roman Baths in Bath.

Not much is known of the of the impact of man in the Cotswolds during the "Dark Ages" because they left little evidence behind, but excavations carried out on Crickley Hill since the 1960's suggest that there may have been a settlement here.

From Medieval times, sheep rearing has been one of main industries in the Cotswolds. Even today you may see the famous Cotswold Lion - an ancient breed of sheep prized for its size and fleece, grazing in local fields. In the Middle Ages the wealth of the area was mostly derived from the wool industry. Evidence of this can be seen in the magnificent churches and buildings in the area funded by the wealthy merchants. Abbeys such as Bath and Hailes also grew rich on the wool trade and the influence of Tewkesbury Abbey stretched as far as Stanway on the Trail where you can still see the workshops and mill.

Cloth manufacture also became a major local industry. It started as a cottage industry but became mechanised with the introduction of the "Spinning Jenny" and "Flying Shuttle". In the Stroud area, Ebley and Stanley are fine examples of mills which manufactured cloth during this period. The development of steam power during the industrial revolution enabled the north of England to become the centre for the textile industry as it had a cheap and plentiful supply of coal. This eventually caused the local industry to decline.

# Landscape and Wildlife

For most of its length the Cotswold Way National Trail runs along the top of the Cotswolds escarpment. This steep escarpment is the exposed edge of the plateau that dips down gently towards the eastern side of the Cotswolds. The underlying oolitic limestone gives the landscape the special value that it has today.

This stone is a valuable building material, and you will pass a number of small disused quarries on the Trail which give a clear insight into the structure of the underlying rock. Some of these quarry faces now provide valuable roosts for rare bats such as the Horseshoe.

The steepness of the scarp slope and extensive common land has helped to protect the now internationally important areas of unimproved calcareous (limestone) grassland. These areas provide a habitat for many species of wild flowers such as orchids, and invertebrates including the Chalkhill Blue butterfly.

The magnificent beech woodlands on the scarp slope have been managed for centuries for timber, charcoal and fire wood. These woodlands can be enjoyed at any time of year with carpets of bluebells and wood anemones in the spring, welcome shade in the summer, rich golden hues in the autumn, and when the leaves fall in the winter, they give way to breathtaking views.

# Preparing for your Walk

### Deciding where to start.

The Cotswold Way can be walked in either direction and is clearly signposted both ways. The route is generally promoted from north to south, starting in Chipping Campden and finishing in Bath. Chipping Campden, being a very fine example of a Cotswolds market town is a good place to start because it gives the walker an immediate taste of the Cotswolds and what is to come whereas Bath with its fine regency architecture and magnificent Abbey, is a wonderful place to finish, and could be viewed as the end of a "pilgrimage".

Another reason is that public transport connections are far less frequent in Chipping Campden than in Bath. Missing your connection home in Chipping Campden could mean an unplanned overnight stay!

### How far to walk in a day.

How far you actually walk in a day is up to you, and depends on your fitness and experience. If you are unsure, it is better to underestimate than over estimate. Usually it is possible to walk 2.5miles (4km) an hour, but on sections with climbs and descents slightly longer should be allowed (and do not be fooled by the Cotswold Way – it has its fair share of these).

### Equipment to take with you

Always make sure that you are properly prepared when you go out for a days walking. Appropriate sturdy footwear is a must as the path may be wet and uneven in places. You will need good waterproofs and extra layers of warm clothing as the weather can change unexpectedly and it is always several degrees colder on the higher sections of the Trail. If you would like to get a local weather report before setting out, see p19.

### Refreshments

Although refreshments are available to buy in places along the trail (see p22) you should always carry plenty to drink and some food to keep your energy up as shops or pubs may be closed, or you may not want to make a detour from the Trail to find them.

### Personal Safety

It is always sensible if you plan to walk alone, to let someone know where you are walking and when you expect to return - a simple precaution insuring that someone can raise the alarm if things do not go as planned. Please bear in mind that mobile phone coverage can be patchy in rural areas so you cannot always rely on them.

# How to get to the Trail

## Public Transport

The Cotswold Way National Trail is generally well served by public transport, however in some locations there is no Sunday service. Comprehensive information is available to help you to plan your walk using public transport:

• **Walk & Explore the Cotswold Way by Public Transport** – a free leaflet on how to get to and from the Cotswold Way from the larger towns in the area. Available to download from the Cotswold Way National Trail web site www.nationaltrail.co.uk, or in hard copy by contacting the Cotswolds Conservation Board ① +44 (0) 1451 862000.

• **Days out and Short Breaks on the Cotswold Way** – free information sheets about how to get to and from sections of the Cotswold Way from Cheltenham, Stroud and Bath. Available to download from the Cotswold Way National Trail web site www.nationaltrail.co.uk.

• **Traveline** – national public transport information ① 0870 608 2608, web site www.traveline.org.uk

## Car Parking

We encourage people to consider using public transport rather than travelling by private car, as this is better for the environment, helps to support local public transport services and also reduces congestion from parking in the smaller settlements.

For those who do wish to use their car, we recommend the most suitable places to park in the route sections in the next part of this guide. Please remember it is always advisable to remove all valuables when leaving your car unattended.

# How to get to the Trail

## Taxi Services

Taxi services are a useful back up to supplement public transport or to get you to accommodation that is some distance from the Trail. The list below is just a selection of the services available in each area and no recommendation is inferred.

**Section 1- Chipping Campden to Broadway** *Cotswold Private Hire* ☎ 01386 840500/07890 857833; *Hedgehog Private hire* (for larger parties) ☎ 01386 430184; *MH Private Car Hire* ☎ 07779 117471; *Four Shires Executive* ☎ 01451 720759; *Cotswold Executive Cars* ☎ 07710 117471; *Ian's Taxis* ☎ 07789 897966, *Transport Solutions West* ☎ 01608 650343

**Section 2 & 3- Broadway to Winchcombe** *Elite Travel* ☎ 01386 853057 / 07917 128114; *Meon Private Hire* ☎ 01386 859078/07765 200237; *Cotswold Horizons* ☎ 01386 858599

**Section 4- Winchcombe to Cleeve Hill** *Amiga Cars* ☎ 01242 603060; *Taylor Private Hire* ☎ 01242 603651

**Section 5- Cleeve Hill to Dowdeswell** *B.J Private Hire* ☎ 01242 674525; *Churchfield Cars* ☎ 01242 676769

**Section 6- Dowdeswell to Leckhampton Hill-** *Prestbury Independent Taxi* ☎ 01242 231362; *Connections Travel* ☎ 01242 239939

**Section 7- Leckhampton Hill to Birdlip** *A 2 B Private Hire (Cheltenham) Ltd* ☎ 01242 580580; *Andycars* ☎ 01242 262611; *A P Taxis* ☎ 01242 699033; *Astra Cabs* ☎ 01242 252233; *Atkins Private Hire* ☎ 07752 036516; *Bridges,* ☎ 01242 706323; *Central Taxis* ☎ 01242 228877; *Cotswold Travel* ☎ 01242 575359; *Spa Cars* ☎ 07968 273164; *Starline Taxis* ☎ 01242 250250; *Tony's Taxi Service* ☎ 01242 260260; *7-2-7 Car Co. Ltd* ☎ 01242 523523

**Section 8- Birdlip to Painswick** *John's Private Hire* ☎ 01452 385050

**Section 9- Painswick to Kings Stanley** *Ted's Cabs* ☎ 01452 813599; *Gardiner Taxis* ☎ 01453 758120; *A-Steve's Taxi* ☎ 01453 752233 / 07980 022586; *Flights Taxis Ltd* ☎ 01453 766138; *Cashes Green Taxi Services* ☎ 01453 753012 / 07779 763228

**Section 10- Kings Stanley to Dursley** *Colin Groves Taxis* ☎ 07968 247891; *Stroud Taxi Co* ☎ 01453 823300; *Dawsons Taxis* ☎ 01453 821493 / 07071 224346; *Stonehouse Taxis* ☎ 01453 822555

**Section 11- Dursley to Wotton under Edge** *Al's Taxi's* ☎ 01453 519354; *A 2 B Taxis* ☎ 01453 548483; *Jenkins Transport* ☎ 01453 542346; *JLD Taxis* ☎ 01453 549595; *C.R Carter* ☎ 01453 543224; *G & K Nash Private Hire* ☎ 01453 547781; *Martin's Taxis* ☎ 01453 548552

**Section 12- Wotton under Edge to Hawkesbury** *Coombe Valley Private Hire Taxis* ☎ 01453 845071

**Section 13- Hawkesbury to Tormarton** *Herbie Hire* ☎ 01454 238379

**Section 14- Tormarton to Cold Ashton** *Beaufort Minibuses & Taxis* ☎ 01454 313721; *Grab-a-Cab* ☎ 01454 889922; *Yate Taxis* ☎ 01454 324747

**Section 15- Cold Ashton to Bath** *Ezee Cab* ☎ 0117 937 3500

# How to follow the Trail

## Signage

The Cotswold Way follows a series of well signed public rights of way and minor roads.
82% of the Trail is off road and the majority of this is on public footpaths.

The acorn is the symbol of National Trails and is used on all of the Cotswold Way signage.
In most cases the signs will also carry the words "Cotswold Way". When on a public right of way
there will also be an indication of the status of the right of way, either in words, or using the
coloured national waymarking symbols. The status indicates who can legally use this section of
path. This is explained below:

# How to follow the Trail

The Official National Trail Guide

**The Cotswold Way** by Anthony Burton, Aurum Press. The official guide to the trail with written route description and colour Ordance Survey maps. Available from book shops price £12.99. ISBN 978 1 84513 9149

Maps

As well as using the National Trail Guide above, it can be helpful to carry the Ordnance Survey maps as these help you to interpret the wider landscape and will assist you in making any detours needed to find refreshments, accommodation or public transport.

Ordnance Survey Explorer Series (1:25,000 scale)
OL45 – The Cotswolds
179 – Gloucester, Cheltenham & Stroud
168 – Stroud, Tetbury & Malmesbury
167 – Thornbury, Dursley & Yate
155 – Bristol & Bath

Ordnance Survey Landranger Series (1:50,000 scale)
151 – Stratford-upon-Avon
150 – Worcester & The Malverns
162 – Gloucester & Forest of Dean
163 – Cheltenham & Cirencester
172 – Bristol & Bath

Route Change Information

The route in the official guide book is correct at the time of going to press. However, there are still some route improvements planned. Details of any further changes will be available as maps to download from the Cotswold Way National Trail webste (www.nationaltrail.co.uk) under "Planning a Trip".

Other Trail Guide Publications

There are other publications available about the Cotswold Way route and related walks. The titles below are just a selection. Please note the publication date because some may show older versions of the route – all of which are still possible to follow but some sections will no longer be signed as the Cotswold Way.

**Cotswold Way Long Distance Route Map** (Harvey 2007) – waterproof map of the entire route. Price £11.95. ISBN 185137342X

**The Cotswold Way** by Kev Reynolds (Cicerone Press 2007) – route description & OS maps in both directions – north to south and south to north. Price £12.00. ISBN 1852844493

**The Cotswold Way** by Mark Richards (Reardon Press 1999) – route description north to south. Wainwright style maps. Price £5.95 ISBN 1873877102

# Tourist Information Providers

**Chipping Campden TIP**
The Old Police Station
High Street
Chipping Campden GL55 6HB
☎+44 (0) 1386 841206
✉ visitchippingcampden@lineone.net
🖱 www.chippingcampden.co.uk

**Broadway TIC**
1 Cotswold Court
Broadway WR12 7AA
☎+44 (0) 1386 852937

**Winchcombe TIC**
Tourist Information Centre
The Town Hall
High Street
Winchcombe GL54 5LJ
☎+44 (0) 1242 602925
(restricted opening hours in winter)

**Cheltenham Spa TIC**
77 The Promenade
Cheltenham GL50 1PJ
☎+44 (0) 1242 522878
🖱 www.visitcheltenham.gov.uk

**Gloucester TIC**
28 Southgate Street
Gloucester GL1 2DP
☎+44 (0) 1452 396572

**Painswick TIP**
The Library
Stroud Road
Painswick GL6 6UT
☎+44 (0) 1452 813522
(seasonal summer opening)

**Stroud TIC**
Subscription Rooms
George Street
Stroud GL5 1AE
☎+44 (0) 1453 760960
🖱 www.stroud.gov.uk

**Wotton under Edge TIP**
Heritage Centre
The Chipping
Wotton under Edge GL12 7AD
☎+44 (0) 1453 521541
🖱 www.wottonheritage.com

**Chipping Sodbury TIC**
The Clock Tower
Chipping Sodbury BS37 6AH
☎+44 (0)1454 888686

**Bath TIC**
Abbey Chambers
Abbey Church Yard
Bath BA1 1LY
☎ (UK callers) 0906 711 2000 (50p/min)
☎ (Overseas callers) +44(0)870 444 6442
🖱 www.visitbath.co.uk

# Organised Holidays and Luggage Carriers

The details of the companies listed below are given for information only and no recommendation is inferred.

## Organised booking and holidays

If you want to organise and book your own accommodation, all the information you need is in the next section of this book. However, if you would like someone to arrange your accommodation for you, or to take you on a guided walk along the trail, there are companies that will organise this for you.

**Celtic Trails** ☎ (UK callers) 0800 970 7585, ☎ (Overseas callers) +44 (0)1600 860846 ⏍ www.celtrail.com
Accommodation booking, luggage transfer, provision of route information

**Compass Holidays** ☎ +44 (0)1242 250642, ⏍ www.compass-holidays.com
Short break guided walking packages including accommodation, covering parts of the Cotswold Way

**Contours Walking Holidays** ☎ +44 (0)1768 867539, ⏍ www.contours.co.uk
Accommodation booking, luggage transfer, provision of route information

**Cotswold Walking Holidays** ☎ +44 (0)1242 633680, ⏍ www.cotswoldwalks.com
Accommodation booking, luggage transfer, provision of route information

**Discovery Travel** ☎ +44 (0)1904 766564, ⏍ www.discoverytravel.co.uk
Offers organised packages including accommodation, covering the whole Cotswold Way

**HF Holidays** ☎ +44 (0)20 8905 9556, ⏍ www.hfholidays.co.uk
Offers 6 day guided walks including accommodation covering 72 miles of the Cotswold Way

**The Sherpa Van Project** ☎ +44 (0)20 8569 4101, ⏍ www.sherpavan.com
Accommodation booking, luggage transfer, provision of route information

**Wycheway Country Walks** ☎ +44 (0)1886 833828, ⏍ www.wychewaycountrywalks.co.uk.
Accommodation booking, luggage transfer, provision of route information

## Luggage Carriers

If you would like to organise your own walk but don't want to carry a heavy pack each day, the following companies offer luggage transfer (full contact details in section above)
**Compass Holidays**
**The Sherpa Van Project**

# Emergency Contacts

We hope you will not need to refer to this page during your walk, but the information below is aimed to help you to find the service that you need quickly and easily should something unforeseen happen. In urgent and life threatening situations or when a crime is in progress the emergency services can be contacted on: **999** or **112**

When the situation is not an emergency please use the following contact numbers:

**Police:**
West Mercia Constabulary ☎ 08457 444888
Gloucestershire Constabulary ☎ 0845 090 1234
Avon & Somerset Constabulary ☎ 01275 818181

**General Health Enquiries**
NHS Direct ☎ 0845 4647

**Hospitals with 24 hour Accident & Emergency cover:**
Worcestershire Royal Hospital, Charles Hastings Way, Newtown Road, Worcester ☎ 01905 763333
Cheltenham General Hospital, Sandford Road, Cheltenham ☎ 08454 222222
Gloucestershire Royal Hospital, Great Western Road, Gloucester ☎ 08454 222222
Bath Royal United Hospital, Combe Park, Bath ☎ 01225 428331
Bristol Frenchay Hospital, Frenchay Park Road, Bristol ☎ 0117 970 1212

# Useful Contacts

### Cotswold Way National Trail Team
Cotswold Way National Trail Office, The Malthouse, Standish, Stonehouse, Gloucestershire, GL10 3DL
☎ +44 (0)1453 827004  ✉ cotsway@gloucestershire.gov.uk  🖱 www.nationaltrail.co.uk

### Highway Authorities responsible for maintaining public rights of way
*Chipping Campden to Kilcott (excluding Broadway)*
Gloucestershire County Council, Public Rights of Way, Environment Department, Shire Hall,
Gloucester, GL1 2TH ☎ +44 (0)1452 425577 ✉ prow@gloucestershire.gov.uk
🖱 www.gloucestershire.gov.uk

*Broadway*
Worcestershire County Council, Countryside Service, County Hall, Spetchley Road, Worcester,
WR5 2XG ☎ +44 (0)1905 768214 ✉ countryside@worcestershire.gov.uk
🖱 www.worcestershire.gov.uk

*Hawkesbury to Cold Ashton (plus the parish of Bitton)*
South Gloucestershire Council, Public Rights of Way, Elliot A1, Broad Lane, Yate, S. Glos. BS37 7ES
☎ +44 (0)1454 863646 ✉ rightsofway@southglos.gov.uk 🖱 www.southglos.gov.uk

*Cold Ashton to Bath (excluding the parish of Bitton)*
Bath and North East Somerset Council, Public Rights of Way, Riverside, Temple Street, Keynsham.
BS31 1LA ☎ +44 (0)1225 477532 ✉ prow@bathnes.gov.uk 🖱 www.bathnes.gov.uk

### *Agency responsible for National Trails*
Natural England, South West Regional Office, 2nd Floor, 11-15 Dix's Field, Exeter, Devon, EX1 1QA
☎ +44 (0)1392 477150 🖱 www.naturalengland.org.uk

### Agency looking after the Cotswolds Area of Outstanding Natural Beauty
Cotswolds Conservation Board, Cotswold Heritage Centre, Northleach, Gloucestershire, GL54 3JH.
☎ +44 (0)1451 862000 🖱 www.cotswoldsaonb.org.uk

### Weather Forecast Information
*Weathercall: (calls 60p/minute)*
*Worcestershire* ☎ 09068 500410
*Gloucestershire & Somerset* ☎ 09068 405415
🖱 www.weathercall.co.uk
*BBC Weather Forecasts*
🖱 www.bbc.co.uk/weather

# Follow the Countryside Code

**Be safe – plan ahead and follow any signs**
Even when going out locally, it's better to get the latest information about where and when you can go. For example, your rights to go onto some areas of open land may be restricted while work is carried out for safety reasons, or during breeding seasons. Follow advice and local signs, and be prepared for the unexpected.

**Leave gates and property as you find them**
Please respect the working life of the countryside, as our actions can affect people's livelihoods, our heritage, and the safety and welfare of animals and ourselves.

**Protect plants and animals, and take your litter home.**
We have a responsibility to protect our countryside now and for future generations, so make sure you don't harm animals, birds, plants or trees.

**Keep dogs under close control**
The countryside is a great place to exercise dogs, but it's every owner's duty to make sure that their dog is not a danger or nuisance to farm animals, wildlife or other people.

**Consider other people**
Showing consideration and respect for other people makes the countryside a pleasant environment for everyone – at home, at work and at leisure.

*For further details visit*
*www.countrysideaccess.gov.uk*

# Accommodation and Local Services

The following chapters give details about the settlements on or near to the Cotswold Way National Trail, with information about accommodation, places to eat and drink, grocery shops, post offices, public conveniences, public telephones, and the best places to park.

The Cotswold Way has been divided into 15 sections (shown on the map on p 5). The sections are listed in geographic, order from the northern end of the Trail (Chipping Campden) to the southern end (Bath).

Please note that the detail given about accommodation and local services in this book does not constitute a recommendation and is for your information only. Where establishments have been awarded a recognised grade(e.g. VisitBritain accommodation standards (★◆)), this will be shown.

## Accommodation

We have a range of accommodation listed in this guide, however, in some of the larger settlements this list is not exhaustive and there will be more available. For further details please contact the local Tourist Information Providers (p16).

Contact details, an indication of the facilities offered and prices are given for each establishment. A key to the symbols used can be found opposite. We strongly recommend that you book accommodation in advance, especially in the smaller settlements where there is less availability. Accommodation in the area will be in high demand during Cheltenham Gold Cup week and other holiday periods. Whilst booking, always check the prices because those quoted here are the minimum charged.

## Local Services

Symbols are used to indicate the local services and facilities available (the key to these can be found opposite). In the smaller settlements, where there are no more than two pubs, the name of establishment and telephone number are given so that you can check in advance whether or not they will be open when you may want to visit for refreshments.

Please remember that in rural areas local post offices and shops may have restricted opening times, so please make sure that you carry enough refreshments for your walk.

# Accommodation and Local Services

## Key to symbols

| | |
|---|---|
| ✦ | Map grid reference |
| 👢 | Shortest walking distance from the Cotswold Way |

### Settlements

| | |
|---|---|
| 📞 | Public Telephone |
| 🚻 | Public Toilets |
| 🍺 | Pub |
| ✉ | Post Office |
| 🛒 | General Store |
| 🫖 | Café / Tea Shop |
| 🍴 | Restaurant |
| 🥡 | Take Away |
| £ | Bank |
| 💳 | Cash Point |
| ✚ | Pharmacy |
| **P P** | Car Parking **Free/Charged** |
| 🚌🚃 | Public Transport Links |
| **TAXI** | Taxi Service Available (see p13) |

### All Accommodation

| | |
|---|---|
| 🐕 | Dogs allowed by arrangement |
| 🔥 | Packed Lunches Available |
| **DRY** | Clothes / Boots drying facilities |
| 🧺 | Outdoor washing facilities |
| 🧺 | Laundry Facilities |
| 🚗 | Transport to and from trail by arrangement |
| 🎒 | Luggage transport to next overnight stop |
| VISA | Credit card(s) accepted |
| 🚶🚶 | Walkers Welcome |
| ❗ | Special feature / comment |

### Accommodation Type

| | |
|---|---|
| ▲ | Hostel |
| ⛺ | Camping |
| 🏠 | Hotel |
| 🏨 | Inn |
| **B&B** | Guest House / Bed & Breakfast |

### Serviced Accommodation

| | |
|---|---|
| 🛏 | Double Room |
| 🛏 | Twin Room |
| 🛏 | Family Room |
| 🛏 | Single Room |
| ⊖ | No Smoking or No Smoking in Bedrooms, check with provider |
| 👪 | Children Welcome |
| ♿ | Wheelchair access |
| V | Caters for Vegetarians |
| 🚫 | Evening meal available at accommodation |
| 📞 | Telephone in accommodation |
| ♦ | Visit Britain accommodation standards for B&B's, guest houses, inns |
| ★ | Visit Britain accommodation standards for hotels |

### Camping

| | |
|---|---|
| ⛺ | Tent Pitches |
| 🚐 | Caravan Pitches |
| 🚰 | Cold Water |
| 🚰 | Hot Water |
| 🚻 | Toilets |
| ♿WC | Toilets adapted for disabled users |
| 🚿 | Showers |
| 📞 | Public telephone |
| 🏪 | Site Shop |
| CG | Camping Gas available |

23

## Section

The journey along the Cotswold Way starts in the beautiful, historic market town of Chipping Campden. After leaving the town the Trail takes you out onto the Cotswold escarpment with stunning views from Dover's Hill where the annual "Olimpick Games" are held. The walk continues across the fields to Broadway Tower and then down into the village of Broadway with its historic connections with the Arts & Crafts movement.

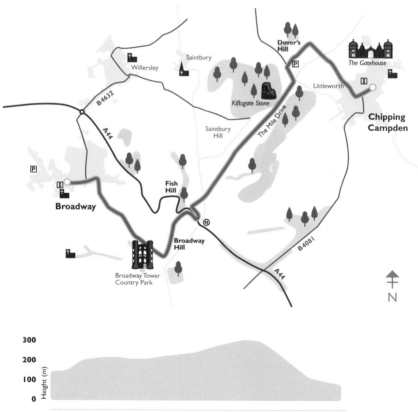

Chipping Campden to Broadway **6mile(s) (9.6 km)**

24

## CHIPPING CAMPDEN

🥾 **on Trail**  **SP150390**

🏨 🛒 🍴 ☕ 🍽 £ 📠 ✚ 📞 ✉ ♿

**TAXI**

🚌 No Sunday Service

P **Back Ends**  **SP152395**

---

### ⓑ Catbrook House

**All year**

★★★★

🥾 **0.3mile(s) (0.5km)**  **SP154384**

*Mrs Anne Klein*

Catbrook, Chipping Campden, Glos, GL55 6DE

**T:** 01386 841499

**M:** 07731 953365

**F:** 01386 849248

**E:** m.klein@virgin.net

**W:** www.chippingcampden.co.uk/catbrook.htm

🛏 2 £52 🛏 1 £62

🚭 👫 (Min 9 years) **V**

Some rooms en-suite

---

### ⓑ Frances Cottage

**Closed Nov - Jan**

🥾 **on Trail**  **SP148390**

*Mrs Jill Slade*

Lower High Street, Chipping Campden, Glos, GL55 6DY

**T:** 01386 840894

**E:** jill.j.slade@btopenworld.com

**W:** www.francescottage.co.uk

🛏 1 £60 🛏 1 £60

🚭 👫 (Min 14 years) **V**

All rooms en-suite

---

### B&B Green Cottage

**All year**

◆◆

🥾 **0.1mile(s) (0.1km)**  **SP145388**

*Mrs Vanessa Ryle*

Park Road, Chipping Campden, Glos, GL55 6EB

**T:** 01386 841428

**W:** www.greencottagebandb.co.uk

🛏 1 £50

🚭 👫 (Min 10 years) **V** DRY

---

### B&B Malt House

**All year**

◆◆◆◆◆

🥾 **1mile(s) (1.6km)**  **SP159377**

*Ms Judi Wilkes*

Broad Campden, Chipping Campden, Glos, GL55 6UU

**T:** 01386 840295

**F:** 01386 841334

**E:** info@malt-house.co.uk

**W:** www.malt-house.co.uk

🛏 6 £128 🛏 1 £150

🚭 👫 📺 **V** DRY 🅾 🚗 🐾

💳 Mastercard, Visa, Amex, Delta

All rooms en-suite

H Quiet picturesque village, one mile from Chipping Campden. Lovely 3 acre English garden, large elegantly furnished bedrooms. Two sitting rooms, summer house and croquet available. Peaceful after a long walk.

# 1    Chipping Campden to Broadway

## B&B Myrtle House

All year

★★★★

⌂ **3.5mile(s) (5.6km)** ᴺ⊕ᴱ **SP161436**

*Ms Kate Rush*

High Street, Mickleton, Chipping Campden,
Glos, GL55 6SA

**T:** 01386 430032

**E:** myrtle@myrtlehouse.co.uk

**W:** www.myrtlehouse.co.uk

🛏 2 £64 🛏 1 £64 🛏 2 £80

🚭 🕇🕇 ▣ V 🚶 DRY 🚗 🥾

 Mastercard, Visa, Delta

All rooms en-suite

## Ⓗ Noel Arms Hotel

All year

★★★

⌂ **on Trail** ᴺ⊕ᴱ **SP150390**

*Mr Seng Loy*

High St, Chipping Campden, Glos,
GL55 6AT

**T:** 01386 840317

**F:** 01386 841136

**E:** reception@noelarmshotel.com

**W:** www.noelarmshotel.com

🛏 10 £130 🛏 13 £130 🛏 1 £180
🛏 2 £90

🚭 🕇🕇 ▣ V 🚶 🌣 🚗 🥾 ☎

 Mastercard, Visa, Amex, Delta

All rooms en-suite

## B&B Sandalwood House

Closed December & January

◆◆◆◆

⌂ **0.1mile(s) (0.1 km)** ᴺ⊕ᴱ **SP143387**

*Mrs Diana Bendall*

Back Ends, Chipping Campden, Glos, GL55 6AU

**T:** 01386 840091

**F:** 01386 840091

🛏 1 £65 🛏 1 £87

🚭 🕇🕇 (Min 10 years) V ▣ ☎

Some rooms en-suite

🛏 Single occupancy £58.

Reductions for weekly stay.

Bottled water / fresh milk / fresh fruit
provided in each room

## B&B Stonecroft B&B

All year

◆◆◆

⌂ **0.3mile(s) (0.5km)** ᴺ⊕ᴱ **SP151390**

*Mr Roger Yates*

George Lane, Chipping Campden, Glos,
GL55 6DA

**T:** 01386 840486

**E:** info@stonecroft-chippingcampden.co.uk

**W:** www.stonecroft-chippingcampden.co.uk

🛏 2 £65 🛏 1 £65

🕇🕇 (Min 12 years) 🥾

All rooms en-suite

🛏 Drying facilities - warm garage is
available

**Taplins**

All year

◆◆◆◆

🛏 **0.3mile(s) (0.5km)** ᴺ⟡ᵉ **SP151398**

*Mrs Rachel Hall*

Taplins, 5 Aston Road, Chipping Campden,
Glos, GL55 6HR.

**T:** 01386 840927
**M:** 07746 742960
**E:** info@cotswoldstay.co.uk
**W:** www.cotswoldstay.co.uk

🛏 1 £55 🛏 1 £55

🚭 ⛄ (min. age 10) 🎿 V DRY 🐾 ▢ 🗺

**The Kings Hotel**

All year

★★★★

🛏 **on Trail** ᴺ⟡ᵉ **SP150391**

*Miss Vanessa Rees*

The Square, Chipping Campden, Glos,
GL55 6AW

**T:** 01386 840256
**E:** info@kingscampden.co.uk
**W:** www.thekingsarmshotel.com

🛏 8 £85 🛏 3 £100

⛄ 🐾 📷 V 🏍 🌑 🚗

🏧 Mastercard, Visa, Amex, Delta
All rooms en-suite

**The Volunteer Inn**

All year

🛏 **on Trail** ᴺ⟡ᵉ **SP149390**

*Mr Mark Gibson*

Lower High Street, Chipping Campden,
Glos, GL55 6DY

**T:** 01386 840688
**F:** 01386 840543
**E:** mark_gibbo@yahoo.co.uk
**W:** www.thevolunteerinn.com

🛏 3 £70 🛏 1 £70 🛏 1 £90

🚭 🐾 ♿ 📷 V 🏍 🌑 🗺

 Mastercard, Visa, Delta
All rooms en-suite

**B&B Weston Park Farm**

All year

◆◆◆

🛏 **0.1mile(s) (0.2km)** ᴺ⟡ᵉ **SP135395**

*Mrs Jane Whitehouse*

Dovers Hill, Chipping Campden, Glos,
GL55 6UW

**T:** 01386 840835
**M:** 07887 550224
**E:** jane_whitehouse@hotmail.com
**W:** www.cotswoldcottages.uk.com

🛏 1 £65 🛏 1 £POA

🐾 V 🏍 DRY 🚗 🗺

All rooms en-suite

## MORETON IN THE MARSH

🛏 **7mile(s) (11km)** ᴺ⟡ᵉ **SP205325**

🍺 🛒 🛍 🫖 🗓 £ ✚ 📞 ✉ 🚶

**TAXI**

🚌 No Sunday bus service to Chipping
Campden

🚂

# 1 Chipping Campden to Broadway

## Fish Hill

👢 **on Trail** ⊕ **SP118371**
🏃
Ⓟ **Fish Hill** ⊕ **SP118371**

## *Section*

From Broadway the Cotswold Way National Trail climbs up onto the escarpment, following broad tracks, to the remains of the Iron Age hill fort of Shenberrow Camp. The Trail then descends into the unspoilt Cotswold village of Stanway. After the village the walking becomes easy across the level farmland of the Stanway Estate, with its Jacobean Manor and the highest gravity fed fountain in Europe. This section finishes in the hamlet of Wood Stanway.

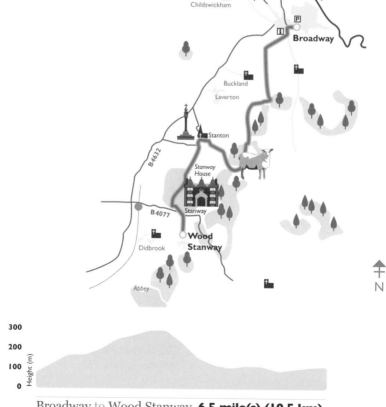

Broadway to Wood Stanway **6.5 mile(s) (10.5 km)**

# 2  Broadway to Wood Stanway

## BROADWAY

🛏 **on Trail**  **SP100375**
🏚 🍴 🫖 🗄 £ 🖼 ✚ 📞 ✉ 👫

**TAXI**
🚌 No Sunday Service
Ⓟ **Leamington Road** ⊕ **SP100377**

### 🅱🅱 Brook House Guest House

**All year**

🛏 **0.4mile(s) (0.7km)** ⊕ **SP090379**
*Mrs Marianne Thomas*
Station Road, Broadway, Worcestershire,
WR12 7DE
**T:** 01386 852313
**M:** 07901 820198
**E:** enquiries@brookhousebroadway.wanadoo.co.uk
**W:** www.brookhousebandb.co.uk
🛏 2 £65 🛏 1 £60 🛏 1 £65 🛏 1 £30
👫 📶 V DRY
Some rooms en-suite

### 🅱🅱 Cowley House

**All year**

◆◆◆◆
🛏 **0.1mile(s) (0.1km)** ⊕ **SP093375**
*Dr Joan Reading*
Church Street, Broadway, Worcestershire,
WR12 7AE
**T:** 01386 858148
**M:** 07778 587803
**E:** cowleyhouse.broadway@tiscali.co.uk
**W:** www.cowleyhouse-broadway.co.uk
🛏 3 £50 🛏 2 £60 🛏 1 £65

🚫 👫 (Min 7 years) 📶 V 🚿 DRY 🚶
📞 🖼
All rooms en-suite

### Ⓗ Dormy House Hotel

**All year**

★★★
🛏 **0.5mile(s) (0.8km)** ⊕ **SP119381**
*Mr Orazio Pollaci*
Willersey Hill, Broadway, Worcestershire,
WR12 7LF
**T:** 01386 852711
**F:** 01386 858636
**E:** oraziop@dormyhouse.co.uk
**W:** www.dormyhouse.co.uk
🛏 22 £160 🛏 14 £160 🛏 8 £210
🛏 1 £120
👫 ♿ 📶 V 🚿 🅾 🚗 🚶
💳 Mastercard, Visa, Amex, Delta
All rooms en-suite

### 🅱🅱 Dove Cottage

**All year**

◆◆◆◆
🛏 **0.1mile(s) (0.1km)** ⊕ **SP101376**
*Ms Delia Holmes*
Colletts Fields, Broadway, Worcestershire,
WR12 7AT
**T:** 01386 859085
**E:** delia.dovecottage@ukonline.co.uk
**W:** www.broadway-cotswolds.co.uk
🛏 1 £60 🛏 1 £60
🚫 🚿 DRY 📺 📞
💳 Mastercard, Visa
All rooms en-suite

## B Mill Hay House

Closed Christmas & New Year

◆◆◆◆◆

🛏 **0.6mile(s) (1km)**  **SP096363**

Mrs Annetta Gorton
Snowshill Road, Broadway, Worcestershire,
WR12 7JS
**T:** 01386 852498
**M:** 07771 541548
**F:** 01386 858038
**E:** millhayhouse@aol.com
**W:** www.millhay.co.uk
🛏 3 £140
🚭 🕴 (Min 12 years) **V** 🌊 **DRY** 📺 🚗 🛴 📞 📷
**VISA** Mastercard, Visa, Delta
All rooms en-suite
🅷 Mill Hay is a Queen Anne country house located in a tranquil setting within easy walking distance of Broadway. The house welcomes a select number of guests to enjoy the luxurious accommodation as a country retreat.

## B Small Talk Lodge

All year

◆◆◆◆

🛏 **on Trail**  **SP097376**

Mr Laurence Avery
32 High Street, Broadway, Worcestershire,
WR12 7DP
**T:** 01386 858953
**M:** 07974 208923
**F:** 01386 858953
**E:** bookings@smalltalklodge.co.uk
**W:** www.smalltalklodge.co.uk
🛏 4 £55 🛏 2 £55 🛏 1 £75

🚭 🕴 **V** 🌊 **DRY** 🛴
**VISA** Mastercard, Visa, Delta, Switch
🅷 Small Talk Lodge is a small friendly family-run guesthouse with a licensed bar and a private car-park

## B&B Southwold House

All year

◆◆◆◆

🛏 **0.4mile(s) (0.6km)**  **SP090379**

Mrs Elvira Mansfield
Station Road, Broadway, Worcestershire,
WR12 7DE
**T:** 01386 853681
**F:** 01386 854610
**W:** www.cotswolds-broadway-southwold.co.uk
🛏 4 £65 🛏 3 £65 🛏 2 £95 🛏 1 £42
🚭 🕴 (Min 5 years) 🍴 📞 **V** 🌊 **DRY** 🚗 🛴
**VISA** Mastercard, Visa, Delta
All rooms en-suite

## H The Broadway Hotel

All year

★★★

🛏 **on Trail**  **SP095374**

Mr Simon Foster
The Green, Broadway, Worcestershire,
WR12 7AA
**T:** 01386 852401
**F:** 01386 853879
**E:** info@broadwayhotel.info
**W:** www.cotswold-inns-hotels.co.uk
🛏 11 £135 🛏 12 £135 🛏 3 £80
🕴 📞 **V** 🌊 🌑 📺 📞
**VISA** Mastercard, Visa

## B&B The Old Stationhouse

All year

◆◆◆◆

 **0.4mile(s) (0.7km)** ʷ⟡ᴱ **SP089383**

*Mrs Pamela Trueman*
Station Drive, Broadway, Worcestershire,
WR12 7DF
**T:** 01386 852659
**E:** oldstationhouse@eastbankbroadway.fsnet.co.uk
**W:** www.broadway-cotswolds.co.uk/oldstationhouse.html
🛏 3 £60 🛏 2 £60 🛏 1 £POA
🚭 ♀♂ (Min 5 years) V 🖤 DRY 🐾 📞
💳 Mastercard, Visa, Delta, Maestro, Switch
All rooms en-suite

## B&B Whiteacres

All year

◆◆◆◆

 **0.5mile(s) (0.8km)** ʷ⟡ᴱ **SP090379**

*Mrs Jenny Buchan*
Station Road, Broadway, Worcestershire,
WR12 7DE
**T:** 01386 852320
**E:** whiteacres@btinternet.com
**W:** www.whiteacres-cotswolds.co.uk
🛏 4 £60 🛏 1 £60
🚭 ♀♂ (Min 10 years) 📺 V DRY 🏠
💳 Mastercard, Visa, Delta, Switch
All rooms en-suite

## B&B Windrush House

All year

★★★★

**0.2mile(s) (0.3km)** ʷ⟡ᴱ **SP092377**

*Mr Evan Anderson*
Station Road, Broadway, Worcestershire,
WR12 7DE
**T:** 01386 853577
**M:** 07717 174339
**F:** 01386 852850
**E:** evan@broadway-windrush.co.uk
**W:** www.broadway-windrush.co.uk
🛏 3 £75 🛏 1 £75
🚭 ♀♂ V 🖤 DRY 🚗 🐾
💳 Mastercard, Visa, Amex, Delta
All rooms en-suite
ℍ 4 Stars Silver Award

## BUCKLAND

**0.5mile(s) (0.8km)** ʷ⟡ᴱ **SP081362**
🗙 📞

## Ⓗ Buckland Manor Hotel

All year

★★★

**0.1mile(s) (0.2km)** ʷ⟡ᴱ **SP081361**

Buckland, Nr Broadway, Worcestershire, WR12 7LY
**T:** 01386 852626
**F:** 01386 853557
**E:** buckland@relaischateaux.com
**W:** www.bucklandmanor.co.uk
🛏 8 £260 🛏 4 £285 🛏 1 £450

**††** (Min 12 years) **⬧ V 🖎 🕲 DRY 🔲 🏃**

 Mastercard, Visa, Amex, Delta

All rooms en-suite

## B Burhill Farm

**All year**

◆◆◆◆◆

🥾 **0.2mile(s) (0.3km)** ᴺ⁺⟡ᴱ **SP083359**

*Mrs Pam Hutcheon*

Buckland, Nr Broadway, Worcestershire,
WR12 7LY

**T:** 01386 858171
**M:** 07891 684377
**F:** 01386 858171
**E:** burhillfarm@yahoo.co.uk
**W:** www.burhillfarm.co.uk

🛏 2 £60

🚫 **†† (10) V 🖎 DRY 🏃**
All rooms en-suite

## SNOWSHILL

🥾 **1.5mile(s) (2.4km)** ᴺ⁺⟡ᴱ **SP096336**
🍺 **Snowshill Arms Inn**
**T:** 01386 852653
🗷 **C**

## B Sheepscombe House

**Closed Christmas**

◆◆◆◆ ★★★★
🥾 **0.3mile(s) (0.5km)** ᴺ⁺⟡ᴱ **SP092336**

*Mrs Jacki Harrison*

Snowshill, Broadway, Worcestershire,
WR12 7JU

**T:** 01386 853769
**M:** 07976 921905
**E:** reservations@snowshill-broadway.co.uk
**W:** www.broadway-cotswolds.co.uk

🛏 1 £75 🛏 1 £75 🛏 1 £POA

🚫 †† 🕿 V 🖎 DRY 🔲 🖼
All rooms en-suite
**H** Visit Britain rating: 4 Stars Gold Award

## STANTON

🥾 **on Trail** ᴺ⁺⟡ᴱ **SP069342**
🍺 **The Mount T:**01386 584316
**C** P **Village Hall** ⟡ᴱ **SP067342**

## B&B Shenberrow Hill

**Closed 20 Dec - 3 Jan**

★★★★
🥾 **on Trail** ᴺ⁺⟡ᴱ **SP071342**

*Mrs Angela Neilan*

Stanton, Nr. Broadway, Worcestershire,
WR12 7NE

**T:** 01386 584468
**M:** 07811 381067
**F:** 01386 584468
**E:** michael.neilan1@btopenworld.com

🛏 2 £70 🛏 2 £70 🛏 1 £90

🚫 †† (Min 7 years) 🕿 V 🖎 DRY 🔲 🏃 C
All rooms en-suite

## B&B The Vine

🛁 **on Trail** ⊕ **SP070341**

*Mrs Jill Carenza*

Stanton, Nr Broadway, Worcestershire,
WR12 7NE

**T:** 01386 584250
**M:** 07074 458425
**F:** 01386 584888
**E:** info@cotswoldsriding.co.uk
**W:** www.cotswoldsriding.co.uk

🛏 1 £60 🛏 1 £60 🛏 1 £75

👫 V 🎿 **DRY** 🔘 👣 🎒

📓 Mastercard, Visa, Delta

Some rooms en-suite

## TODDINGTON ROUNDABOUT

🛁 **0.9mile(s) (1.5km)** ⊕ **SP048324**

🍺 **Pheasant Inn T:** 01242 621271

🧺 🍽 📞

🚌 No Sunday Service

🚂 Gloucestershire & Warwickshire
Steam Railway seasonal service

# Section

## Wood Stanway to Winchcombe

### 5.4 mile(s) (8.8 km)

This section starts with a steep climb up from Wood Stanway onto the escarpment where you will be rewarded by magnificent views across the vale of Evesham towards the Malverns. Passing the Iron Age hillfort of Beckbury Camp, you then descend to Hailes, with its ruined abbey and little church. The Cotswold Way continues through farmland into the Cotswold town of Winchcombe along the curiously named Puckpit Lane.

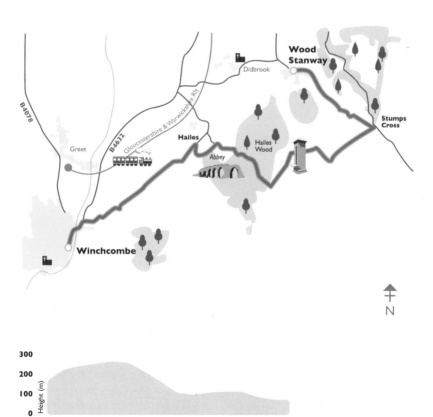

Wood Stanway to Winchcombe **5.4 mile(s) (8.8 km)**

35

# 3    Wood Stanway to Winchcombe

## WOOD STANWAY

**on Trail** ⊕ **SP063312**
🚌 No Sunday Service
🚂 Gloucestershire & Warwickshire
Steam Railway seasonal service
🚫 **Please do not try to park here**

### B&B Gantier

Closed Christmas and New Year

◆◆◆◆
**3.7mile(s) (6km)** ⊕ **SP003333**
*Mrs Sue Parry*
12 Church Road, Alderton,
Tewkesbury, Glos, GL20 8NR
**T:** 01242 620343
**M:** 07787 504872
**E:** johnandsueparry@yahoo.co.uk
**W:** www.gantier.co.uk
🛏 2 £50 🛏 1 £30
🚭 🕺 🗻 🌑 DRY 🔲 🚗 👣 🖼
All rooms en-suite

### B&B Glebe Farm

Closed Christmas
**on Trail** ⊕ **SP063312**
*Mrs Ann Flavell-Wood*
Wood Stanway, Cheltenham, Glos,
GL54 5PG
**T:** 01386 584791
**E:** emma@woodstanway.co.uk
**W:** www.woodstanway.co.uk
🛏 1 £32 🛏 2 £28
🕺 V 🗻 🌑 DRY 🔲 🚗 🖼

🔳 Mastercard, Visa
All rooms en-suite

### B&B Wood Stanway Farmhouse

All year

**on Trail** ⊕ **SP062311**
*Mrs Margaret Green*
Wood Stanway, Nr. Winchcombe, Glos,
GL54 5PG
**T:** 01386 584318
**E:** greensbedandbreakfast@hotmail.com
**W:** www.woodstanwayfarmhouse.co.uk
🛏 1 £55 🛏 1 £55 🛏 1 £55
🚭 🕺 V 🗻 🌑 DRY 👣
All rooms en-suite

## HAILES

**on Trail** ⊕ **SP052300**
☕

### 🏕 Hayles Fruit Farm

All year
**on Trail** ⊕ **SP053298**
*Mr M Harrell*
Winchcombe, Nr Cheltenham, Glos, GL54 5PB
**T:** 01242 602123
**F:** 01242 603320
**E:** info@hayles-fruit-farm.co.uk
**W:** www.hayles-fruit-farm.co.uk
🏕 6 £4 per person per night 🚐 6 £11.50
per caravan (2 people)
🕺 🔲 🔲 ⊕ 🚻 WC 🔥 🗑 🔳 CG

Mastercard, Visa, Delta
A rural site on Cotswold Way, next to Hailes Abbey. Electric hook-ups, toilet, shower, farmshop, tearoom

## North Farmcote B & B

All year

★★★★

🥾 **0.3mile(s) (0.5km)** N–S **SP062289**

*Mr David Eayrs*

North Farmcote, Winchcombe, Glos, GL54 5AU

**T:** 01242 602304

**M:** 07792 328274

**E:** davideayrs@yahoo.co.uk

**W:** www.glosfarmhols.co.uk/north-farmcote/index.htm

🛏 1 £55  2 £55  1 £70

🚫 ⚤ ⚤ 📱 V DRY ⊚ 🚗 📷

All rooms en-suite

*Section*

## Winchcombe to Cleeve Hill

### 5.6 mile(s) (9 km)

The Cotswold Way National Trail leaves Winchcombe through the Sudeley estate, climbing steadily along field paths up to the ancient Neolithic long barrow of Belas Knap. The route then follows broad tracks to the edge of Cleeve Common – a Site of Special Scientific Interest, protected for its calcareous grassland species. The Trail crosses the common, passing an historic washpool before climbing again to the Golf Club House at Cleeve Hill.

Winchcombe to Cleeve Hill **5.6 mile(s) (9 km)**

## WINCHCOMBE

**⛺ on Trail** ⌖ **SP024285**

🏠🏪🍴☕🏧💷🏡➕📞✉️👥**TAXI**

🚂 No Sunday Service

🚂 Gloucestershire & Warwickshire Steam Railway seasonal service

Ⓟ **Back Lane** ⌖ **SP023284**

---

### B Blair House

Closed Christmas

◆◆◆◆

⛺ **1.2mile(s) (2km)** ⌖ **SP032287**

*Mrs Sarah Chisholm*

41 Gretton Road, Winchcombe, Glos, GL54 5EG

**T:** 01242 603626

**F:** 01242 604214

**E:** chissurv@aol.com

🛏️ 1 £52 🛏️ 1 £50 🛏️ 1 £30

🚭 ⚥ V **DRY** 🔲 🖼️

Some rooms en-suite

---

### B Cleevely

★★★★

⛺ **0.1mile(s) (0.2km)** ⌖ **SP022266**

*Mrs Carole Rand*

Corndean Lane, Winchcombe, Glos, GL54 5AL

**T:** 01242 602059

🛏️ 1 £50 🛏️ 1 £60

🚭 ⚥ ♙ V 🐾 🌙 **DRY** 🥾

All rooms en-suite

---

### B&B Gaia Cottage

Closed 24 Dec - 1 Jan

◆◆◆◆

⛺ **0.2mile(s) (0.4km)** ⌖ **SP021282**

*Mr Brian Simmonds*

50 Gloucester St, Winchcombe, Glos, GL54 5LX

**T:** 01242 603495

**M:** 07815 104285

**E:** briansimmonds@onetel.com

🛏️ 1 £55 🛏️ 1 £55

🚭 ⚥ V 🐾 **DRY**

---

### B&B Gower House

Closed Christmas and New Year

◆◆◆◆

⛺ **0.1mile(s) (0.1km)** ⌖ **SP025284**

*Mrs Sally Simmonds*

16 North Street, Winchcombe, Glos, GL54 5LH

**T:** 01242 602616

**M:** 07811 387495

**E:** gowerhouse16@aol.com

🛏️ 1 £52 🛏️ 2 £55

🚭 ⚥ 🐾 **DRY** 🥾

Some rooms en-suite

🏠 17th century town house close to pubs, restaurants and shops in town centre.

Single occupancy of rooms £38

## B&B Greenhyde

All year

◆◆◆◆

⌂ **0.5mile(s) (0.8km)**  **SP017281**

*Mrs Dora Wigg*

Langley Road, Winchcombe, Glos, GL54 5QP

**T:** 01242 602569

🛏 1 £54 🛏 1 £52

🚭 👭 V 🐾 DRY 🗗 📞

Some rooms en-suite

🔪 Comfortable with most facilities. Excellent local sourced food, large garden overlooking clear view to fields and hills, 5 min from excellent pub meals. Private sitting room. Plenty of breakfast choice.

## B&B Isbourne Manor House

Closed Christmas

◆◆◆◆◆

⌂ **on Trail**  **SP028284**

*Mrs Felicity King*

Castle Street, Winchcombe, Glos, GL54 5JA

**T:** 01242 602281

**F:** 01242 602281

**E:** felicity@isbourne-manor.co.uk

**W:** www.isbourne-manor.co.uk

🛏 2 £80 🛏 1 £70

🚭 👭 V DRY 🗗 🚗 🖐 📞 🖼

Some rooms en-suite

## B&B Manor Farm

🅰 Closed Christmas

◆◆◆◆

⌂ **0.9mile(s) (1.5km)**  **SP025300**

*Mr Richard Day*

Greet, Winchcombe, Glos, GL54 5BJ

**T:** 01242 602423

**F:** 01242 602423

🛏 2 £60 🛏 1 £60 🅰 6 £5 🚐 4 £8

👭 ♿ DRY 📖 📞 🚰 🐾 🛝

💳 Mastercard, Visa, Delta

All rooms en-suite

🔪 Working farm - manor house - 1 mile Winchombe shops. 150 yds from public house

## B&B Mercia Guest House

Closed Christmas

★★★★

⌂ **on Trail** **SP026284**

*Mrs Jean Upton*

Hailes Street, Winchcombe, Glos, GL54 5HU

**T:** 01242 602251

**F:** 01242 609206

**E:** mercia@uk2.net

**W:** www.merciaguesthouse.co.uk

🛏 3 £54 🛏 1 £54

🚭 👭 🖼 V 🐾 DRY 🖐 🖼

All rooms en-suite

🔪 A warm welcome awaits visitors in this grade II listed 500 year old cottage on the Cotswold Way. Private car parking. Full fire certificate. Near all amenities.

## B&B Old Station House

All year

★★★★

⌂ **1.2mile(s) (1.8km)** **SP025298**

*Mrs Jennifer Collier*

Greet, Winchcombe, Glos, GL54 5LD

**T:** 01242 602283

**F:** 01242 602283
**E:** old_station_house@hotmail.com
🛏 2 £50 🛏 1 £60
⊘ ⚤ V ⚘ DRY ☉ 🚶 ▦
Some rooms en-suite

## Old White Lion Inn

**All year**

🏠 **0.3mile(s) (0.5km)** ᴺ🧭 **SP024284**
*Mr Jason Hobbs*
37 North Street, Winchcombe, Glos, GL54 5PS
**T:** 01242 603300
**E:** jason@theoldwhitelion.com
**W:** www.theoldwhitelion.com
🛏 3 £60 🛏 2 £60 🛏 2 £38
⊘ ⚤ ⚤ ▣ V ⚘ ◐ DRY ☉ 🚶 ☎
 Mastercard, Visa, Amex, Delta
All rooms en-suite
⚑ 15th century coaching inn, oldest in Winchcombe

## One Silk Mill Lane

**Closed 24 Dec - 1 Jan**

◆◆◆◆
🏠 **on Trail** ᴺ🧭 **SP026283**
*Mrs Jenny Cheshire*
Winchcombe, Glos, GL54 5HZ
**T:** 01242 603952
**M:** 07748 318848
**E:** jenny.cheshire@virgin.net
🛏 2 £50
⊘ ⚤ ⚤ V ⚘ DRY ☉ 🚗 🚶
All rooms en-suite

## B&B Parks Farm

**Closed Nov to end of April**

★★★★
🏠 **1.2mile(s) (2km)** ᴺ🧭 **SP046265**
*Mrs Rosemary Wilson*
Sudeley, Winchcombe, Glos, GL54 5JB
**T:** 01242 603874
**M:** 07833 561793
**F:** 01242 603874
**E:** rosemaryawilson@hotmail.com
**W:** www.parksfarm.co.uk
🛏 2 £50
⊘ ⚤ (Min 4 years) ▣ V DRY ☉ ▦
⚑ Cotswold hills farm, 3 miles from Winchcombe. Good as a base for walking. Own car or taxi or cycle necessary. (1.5 miles up farm track)

## INN The Plaisterers Arms

**Closed 24 &25 Dec**

🏠 **0.1mile(s) (0.2km)** ᴺ🧭 **SP024282**
*Ms Elizabeth McClintock*
Abbey Terrace, Winchcombe, Glos, GL54 5LL
**T:** 01242 602358
**F:** 01242 602360
**E:** plaisterers.arms@btinternet.com
**W:** www.plaisterersarms.com
🛏 2 £55 🛏 2 £55 🛏 2 £75 🛏 2 £35
⊘ ⚤ ♿ ▣ V ⚘ ◐ DRY 🚗 🚶 ☎
Mastercard, Visa, Delta
All rooms en-suite

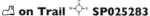 **Wesley House**

Closed 25 &26 Dec

◆◆◆◆

🥾 **on Trail** ⊕ **SP025283**

*Mr Matthew Brown*

High Street, Winchcombe, Glos, GL54 5LJ

**T:** 01242 602366

**F:** 01242 609046

**E:** enquiries@wesleyhouse.co.uk

**W:** www.wesleyhouse.co.uk

🛏 4 £80 🛏 1 £80

🚫 ✝ V 🔥 🅝 [DRY] 🔲 🚗 🔌 📞

[VISA] Mastercard, Visa, Amex

All rooms en-suite

🅷 15th century building. New wine and tapas bar open next door so meals can be taken there as well as in the restaurant.

## Section

# Cleeve Hill to Dowdeswell

### 5.5 mile(s) (8.9 km)

Heading south from Cleeve Hill, you are now on the highest part of the Trail (317m at the Trig Point). The Trail continues across Cleeve Common with extensive views over Cheltenham and beyond. The Cotswold Way then passes through Bill Smylie's butterfly reserve and on to quiet lanes, before starting the descent through Dowdeswell Wood to the reservoir – one of the few places where the rare native white clawed crayfish can still be found.

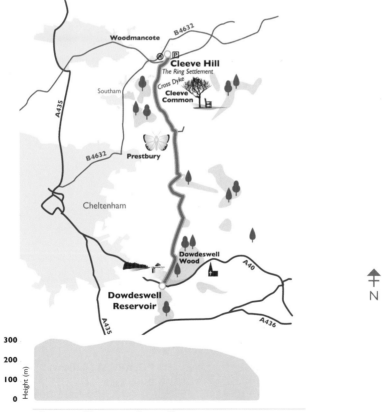

Cleeve Hill to Dowdeswell **5.5 mile(s) (8.9 km)**

43

# 5　Cleeve Hill to Dowdeswell

## CLEEVE HILL

🛏 **0.3mile(s) (0.5km)** ⌖ **SO982268**
🏠 **Rising Sun Hotel**
**T:**01242 676281
📻 📞 🚹 **TAXI**
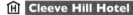

P **Cleeve Hill quarry** ⌖ **SP989271**

### 🏨 Cleeve Hill Hotel

**All year**

◆◆◆◆◆
🛏 **0.1mile(s) (0.2km)** ⌖ **SO987269**
*Mrs Joanne Ogden*
Cleeve Hill, Cheltenham, Glos, GL52 3PR
**T:** 01242 672052
**F:** 01242 679969
**E:** info@cleevehill-hotel.co.uk
**W:** www.cleevehill-hotel.co.uk
🛏 6 £75 🛏 2 £60 🛏 1 £45
🚭 ⚤ (Min 8 years) V 🔥 DRY 🐾 📞
💳 Mastercard, Visa, Amex, Delta
All rooms en-suite
H Free tea and cake on arrival, very warm welcome

### 🏨 Hacketts at The Malvern View

**Closed first 2 weeks of Jan**

◆◆◆◆◆
🛏 **0.3mile(s) (0.5km)** ⌖ **SO984268**
*Mr Paul Hackett*
Cleeve Hill, Cheltenham, Glos, GL52 3PR
**T:** 01242 672017
**F:** 01242 672031

**E:** enquiries@malvernviewhotel.co.uk
**W:** www.malvernviewhotel.co.uk
🛏 3 £80 🛏 1 £80
🚭 ⚤ V 🔥 🐾 DRY 📻 🐾 🎣
💳 Mastercard, Visa, Delta
All rooms en-suite

### B&B Monks Rest

**All year**

🛏 **0.6mile(s) (1km)** ⌖ **SO968256**
*Mrs Alison Bennett*
Southam Lane, Cheltenham, Glos, GL52 3NY
**T:** 01242 514277
🛏 2 £20
🚭 V 🔥 🐾 DRY 📻 🚗 🎣

### B&B Pigeon House Cottage

**Closed Christmas**

🛏 **0.9mile(s) (1.5km)** ⌖ **SO973255**
*Mrs Barbara Holden*
Southam Lane, Southham, Glos, GL52 3NY
**T:** 01242 584255
**E:** barbara.jholden@tiscali.co.uk
**W:** www.pigeonhousecottage.co.uk
🛏 1 £60 🛏 2 £60
🚭 ⚤ V 🔥 DRY 📻 🚗 🎣
H Situated within a pretty cotswold farmstead, adjacent to tythe barn and 12c church - good local pubs - lift to and fro by owner.

### 🏨 Rising Sun Hotel

**All year**

★★
🛏 **0.2mile(s) (0.4km)** ⌖ **SO981268**
*Mr Parviz Tabai*

Cleeve Hill, Cheltenham, Glos, GL52 3PX
**T:** 01242 529671
**W:** www.risingsunhotel.com
14 £90 4 £90 2 £105
3 £70 V DRY
Mastercard, Visa, Amex, Delta
All rooms en-suite
Wireless internet connection to some rooms. All prices frequently subject to special offers.

## B Whittington Lodge Farm

**Closed 21 Dec - 28 Feb**

◆◆◆◆
**1.4mile(s) (2.2km) SP011213**
*Mrs Cathy Boyd*
Whittington , Cheltenham, Glos, GL54 4HB
**T:** 01242 820603
**M:** 07976 691589
**F:** 01242 820603
**E:** cathy@whittlodgefarm.fslife.co.uk
**W:** www.whittlodgefarm.fslife.co.uk
1 £60 2 £60
(Min 12 years) V DRY
All rooms en-suite
Transport available to local pub for evening meal

## PRESTBURY

**1mile(s) (1.6km) SO974238**
**Kings Arms T:** 01242 244403
£ + TAXI

## B&B 43 Welland Lodge Road

**All year**

**1.7mile(s) (2.8km) SO961266**
*Mrs Joy Sagar*
Cheltenham, Glos, GL52 3HB
**T:** 01242 578314
**E:** joysagar@tiscali.co.uk
1 £POA 1 £25
(Min 5 years) V DRY

# Section

## Dowdeswell to Leckhampton Hill

### 4.7 mile(s) (7.6 km)

From Dowdeswell, the Cotswold Way National Trail passes through Lineover Wood – a semi-natural broadleaved woodland, notable amongst other things for its large leaved lime trees. The route then climbs up to Wistley Plantation and on over farmland before descending to pass close to Severn Springs (believed by some to be the source of the Thames). From Severn Springs the path climbs again onto Charlton Kings Common with its magnificent views across Cheltenham and the Severn Vale and then follows the escarpment onto Leckhampton Hill – look out for the distinctive outcrop of rock known locally as Devil's Chimney.

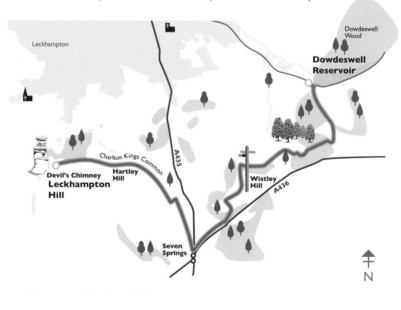

Dowdeswell to Leckhampton Hill **4.7 mile(s) (7.6 km)**

## DOWDESWELL RESEVOIR

⛺ **on Trail** ⊕ **SO986196**
🍺 **Resevoir Inn T:**01242 529671
🚌

Ⓟ **Resevoir Inn (by kind permission of landlord)** ⊕ **SO986197**

### Langett

*Closed Christmas*

⛺ **on Trail** ⊕ **SO988198**
*Mrs Jennifer Cox*
Cotswold Way, London Road,
Cheltenham, Glos, GL54 4HG
**T:** 01242 820192
**F:** 01242 820192
**E:** cox.langett@btopenworld.com
🛏 1 £52 🛏 1 £52
🚭 ♟ V 🔥 DRY 🔲 🚗 🐾 📷
🍴 Hot & Cold Drinks available in the Tea Garden. Adjacent to Dowdeswell Reservoir. Single occupancy of rooms £31

### Reservior Inn

*Closed Mondays*

⛺ **on Trail** ⊕ **SO987197**
*Mr Damien Doebelin*
Charlton Kings, Cheltenham,
Glos, GL54 4HG
**T:** 01242 529671
🛏 1 £50 🛏 2 £50
♟ V 🔥 🛑 DRY 🔲
💳 Mastercard, Visa, Amex, Delta

## CHARLTON KINGS

⛺ **1 mile(s) (1.6km)** ⊕ **SO972206**
🍺 **Duke of York T:**01242 576789
🍺 **Charlton Kings Hotel T:**01242 231061
🛒 🎁 ➕ 📞

### B&B California Farm

*Closed Christmas holidays*

⛺ **0.2mile(s) (0.25km)** ⊕ **SO979188**
*Mrs Lynne Bennett*
Capel Lane, Charlton Kings, Cheltenham,
Glos, GL54 4HQ
**T:** 01242 244746
🛏 2 £60 🛏 2 £60
🚭 ♟ (Min 4 years) ♿ V 🔥 🛑 DRY 🔲 📷

### H Charlton Kings Hotel

*All year*

★★★
⛺ **0.6mile(s) (1km)** ⊕ **SO977201**
*Mr Michael Ebert*
London Road, Cheltenham, Glos, GL52 6UU
**T:** 01242 231061
**M:** 07860 215171
**F:** 01242 241900
**E:** enquiries@charltonkingshotel.co.uk
**W:** www.charltonkingshotel.co.uk
🛏 6 £95 🛏 4 £120 🛏 1 £120 🛏 2 £65
🚭 ♟ ♿ 📺 V 🔥 🛑 DRY 🔲 📞
💳 Mastercard, Visa, Amex, Delta, JCB, Solo
All rooms en-suite
🍴 Privately owned

# 6     Dowdeswell to Leckhampton Hill

## B&B Cotswold Studio

All year

⛰ **0.9mile(s) (1.5km)** ⊕ **SO967207**

*Mrs Geraldine White*
22 Ledmore Rd, Charlton Kings,
Cheltenham, Glos, GL53 8RA
**T:** 01242 526957
**E:** geraldine.white@btinternet.com
**W:** www.cotswoldstudio.co.uk

🛏 I £50 ⛵ I £50 🚗 I £25
🚭 ⛹ V 🌡 DRY 🔲 🚗 🐾 🔲

All rooms en-suite

## B&B Detmore House

All year

★★★

⛰ **0.9mile(s) (1.4km)** ⊕ **SO977201**

*Mrs Gill Kilminster*
London Road, Charlton Kings,
Cheltenham, Glos, GL52 6UT
**T:** 01242 582868
**E:** gillkilminster@breathemail.net
**W:** www.detmorehouse.com

🛏 I £55 ⛵ I £55 ⛵ I £65
🚭 ⛹ 🔲 V

All rooms en-suite

## B&B Hilden Lodge

All Year

⛰ **1.6mile(s) (2.5km)** ⊕ **SO968206**

*Mr Gavin Atkinson*
271 London Road, Charlton Kings, Glos,
GL52 6YG.
**T:** 01242 583242
**F:** 01242 263511

**E:** info@hildenlodge.co.uk
**W:** www.hildenlodge.co.uk

🛏 2 £69 ⛵ 4 £69 ⛵ I £85 🚗 2 £49
🚭 ⛹ (3 years) V 🌡 DRY 🚗 🐾 🔲

VISA Mastercard, Visa, American Express,
AMEX 2% surcharge
All rooms en-suite
⛴ Rating applied for

## SEVERN SPRINGS

⛰ **0.2mile(s) (0.3km)** ⊕ **SO967169**
🍺 **The Severn Springs**
**T:** 01242 870219
🚌 No Sunday Service
Ⓟ **Layby on A436** ⊕ **SO969172**

## Needlehole Forge

B&B All year

⛰ **0.8mile(s) (1.3km)** ⊕ **SO983167**

*Mrs Anne Partridge*
Hilcot, Upper Coberley,
Cheltenham, Glos, GL53 9RD
**T:** 01242 870531
**M:** 07768 130598
**E:** partridge.solutions@virgin.net

🛏 I £50 ⛵ I £50 🚗 I £25
🚭 ⛹ 🔲 V 🌡 Ⓝ DRY 🔲 🚗 🐾 🔲

⛴ Dedicated bathroom to rooms

## Section

## Leckhampton Hill to Birdlip

### 5.6 mile(s) (9 km)

After leaving Leckhampton Hill, the Cotswold Way follows quiet tracks, lanes and paths into Crickley Hill Country Park, with its excellent view points, and information about the archaeological finds from the site that indicate many periods of occupation. The Trail then crosses the undulating grassland of Barrow Wake, before heading into the woods to emerge at Birdlip.

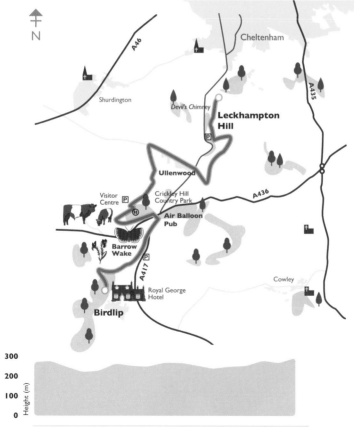

Leckhampton Hill to Birdlip **5.6 mile(s) (9 km)**

## LECKHAMPTON HILL

🏕 **on Trail** ᴺ⌖ **SO946176**
Ⓟ **Quarry, Hartley Lane** ⌖ **SO946176**

## LECKHAMPTON

🏕 **0.8mile(s) (1.3km)** ᴺ⌖ **SO948199**
🍺 **Wheatsheaf Inn**
**T:**01242 525371
🛒 📞
🚌

**B&B** 47 Collum End Rise
All year

🏕 **0.6mile(s) (1km)** ᴺ⌖ **SO947195**
*Mrs Shelagh Hallaway*
Leckhampton,
Cheltenham, Glos, GL53 0PA
**T:** 01242 576574
**E:** shelagh_hallaway@yahoo.co.uk
🛏 1 £45 🛏 1 £66 🛏 1 £23
🚭 👫 (Min 5 years) **V** 🔥 🌙 **DRY** 🔘 🖼
**H** We are experienced walkers ourselves and RA members. We offer accommodation to walkers in a family home

## B&B Sundown

All year

★★★
🏕 **0.5mile(s) (0.8km)** ᴺ⌖ **SO918174**
*Mrs Anna Atkins*
Whitelands Lane, Little Shurdington, Glos, GL51 4TX
**T:** 01242 863353
**M:** 07719 539118
🛏 2 £50 🛏 1 £50 🛏 1 £25
👫 ♿ 🐕 📺 **V** 🔥 🌙 **DRY** 🔘 🖼
All rooms en-suite
**H** Relaxed accommodation located in village - very peaceful. Home-cooked quality food. Outstanding natural beauty. Beautiful views. Tea making facilities. Colour TV.

## CRICKLEY HILL COUNTRY PARK

🏕 **on Trail** ᴺ⌖ **SO930164**
🚻
Ⓟ **Crickley Hill Country Park**
⌖ **SO930164**

## AIR BALLOON ROUNDABOUT

🏕 **on Trail** ᴺ⌖ **SO935162**
🍺 **The Air Balloon T:**01452 862541
📞

## Crickley Court Guest House

All year

★★★★

 **0.6mile(s) (0.9km)** <sup>N</sup> **SO920158**

*Mr Geoffrey Pilgrim-Morris*
Dog Lane, Witcombe, Glos, GL3 4UF
**T:** 01452 863634
**M:** 07919 856218
**F:** 01452 863634
**E:** lispilgrimmorris@yahoo.co.uk

2 £70  2 £70

Mastercard, Visa, Delta

All rooms en-suite

Crickley Court B&B offers a friendly welcome, comfortable house and good breakfast!

## Greenhatch Farm

Closed Christmas

**0.6mile(s) (1km)** <sup>N</sup> **SO962147**

*Lindsay Baker*
Cowley, Cheltenham, Glos, GL53 9NJ
**T:** 01242 870237
**M:** 07768 054996
**F:** 01242 870237
**E:** lindsaybaker@waitrose.com

1 £55

(Min 10 years)

All rooms en-suite

Comfortable, newly decorated double room on ground floor. Idyllic rural situation just 1.5 miles from junction A417/A436 (can pick up from there). Evening meal available and near four pubs with real ale and good food (can offer lifts).

## B&B Springfields Farm

Closed Christmas

◆◆◆

**1.5mile(s) (2.4km)** <sup>N</sup> **SO908158**

*Miss Joyce Bickell*
Little Witcombe, Glos, GL3 4TU
**T:** 01452 863532

1 £40  1 £40  1 £20  1 £5

## BARROW WAKE

**on Trail** <sup>N</sup> **SO931154**
**P Barrow Wake** <sup>N</sup> **SO931154**

## Section

## Birdlip to Painswick

### 8.6 mile(s)(13.9 km)

From Birdlip, the Trail passes through magnificent ancient, semi-natural beech woodlands. Look out for the sign that points out a short detour that can be taken to visit Witcombe Roman Villa. At Coopers Hill the Trail passes the top of the steep slope where the annual cheese rolling event takes place before continuing into the National Nature Reserve at Buckholt wood. The Trail then emerges onto the common land and golf course of Painswick Beacon where Kimsbury Camp, an Iron Age Hillfort with its clearly visible ramparts can be seen. This section ends in the picturesque Cotswold town of Painswick.

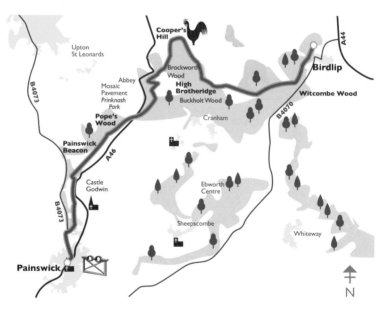

Birdlip to Painswick  **8.6 mile(s) (13.9km)**

## BIRDLIP

 **0.25mile(s) (0.4km)** <sup>N</sup> **SO927144**

🍺 **The Royal George Hotel**

**T:** 01452 862506

📞

🚌 No Sunday Service

### B Highcroft

**Closed 19-26 Dec**

**1.4mile(s) (2.25km)** <sup>N</sup> **SO938125**

*Mrs Christine Butler*

Highcroft, Brimpsfield, Glos, GL4 8LF

**T:** 01452 862405

**M:** 07976 939888

🛏️ 1 £60

🚭 ♿ V 🔥 DRY 📷 🚗 🐾 🖼️

All rooms en-suite

🍴 Will take to local pub for evening meal and collect

### Royal George Hotel

**All year**

**0.1mile(s) (0.2km)** <sup>N</sup> **SO926143**

*Mr Martin Gormley*

Birdlip, Gloucestershire, Glos, GL4 8JH

**T:** 01452 862506

**W:** www.theroyalgeorge-hotel.com

🛏️ 17 £95  🛏️ 7 £95  🛏️ 3 £105

🚭 ♿ V 🔥 🌓 DRY 📷 🐾

💳 Mastercard, Visa, Amex, Delta

All rooms en-suite

## 🏕️ The Haven Tea Garden

**Open throughout the summer**

🏕️ **on Trail** <sup>N</sup> **SO894147**

*Mrs Hellerman*

Coopers Hill, Gloucester, Glos, GL3 4SB

**T:** 01452 863213

🏕️ 8 £5

♿ 🖼️ 📖 🧑 🔥 🚰

## CRANHAM

**0.6mile(s) (1.1km)** <sup>N</sup> **SO897130**

🍺 **The Black Horse T:** 01452 812217

### B&B Pound Cottage

**Closed Christmas and New Year**

**1.2mile(s) (2km)** <sup>N</sup> **SO897130**

*Mrs Milly Dann*

Cranham, Gloucester, Glos, GL4 8HP

**T:** 01452 812581

**F:** 01452 814380

**E:** ddann@globalnet.co.uk

🛏️ 1 £56  🛏️ 1 £56

🚭 ♿ V 🔥 DRY 📷 🚗 🐾

🍴 Local pub closed Sunday and Monday (No evening meal)

## PRINKNASH ABBEY

**0.6mile(s) (1km)** <sup>N</sup> **SO880135**

🫖

# 8 Birdlip to Painswick

## CRANHAM CORNER

🚶 **0.1mile(s) (0.15km)** ⊕ **SO878127**
🍺 **The Royal William T:**01452 813650

## Section

# Painswick to Kings Stanley

## 7.8 mile(s) (12.6 km)

The Cotswold Way descends from Painswick to cross the Wash Brook before climbing again onto Edge Common – an open area of limestone grassland with views back over Painswick. The Trail then plunges back into the woodland, emerging at Haresfield Beacon, an Iron Age hillfort with views of the escarpment and River Severn. The topograph on nearby Shortwood helps to interpret the landscape and views. The route now descends gently through Standish Woods, with beautiful displays of bluebell and wood anemone in the spring to emerge into the Stroud Valleys through grass pastures. At the Stroudwater Navigation at Ryeford, there is a choice of route. One option is to take the route alongside the canal and up over Selsley Common, and the other is to take the route via Kings Stanley.

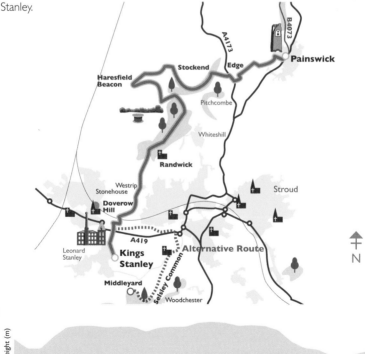

Painswick to Kings Stanley **7.8 mile(s) (12.6 km)**

# 9   Painswick to Kings Stanley

## PAINSWICK

🥾 **on Trail** ⌖ **SO866096**
🏚 **The Falcon Inn T:**01452 814222
🏚 **The Royal Oak T:**01452 813129
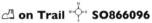 **TAXI**

P **Painswick Walkers Car Park**
⌖ **SO868105**

---

B&B **3 Painswick Heights**

All year

🥾 **0.9mile(s) (1.5km)** ⌖ **SO873086**
*Miss Patricia Moroney*
Yokehouse Lane, Painswick, Glos, GL6 7QS
**T:** 01452 812347
**M:** 07850 212052
**E:** bsimplybetter@tiscali.co.uk
🛏 1 £55 🛏 1 £55
🚭 V 🔥 🌢 DRY 🚗
Some rooms en-suite

---

B&B **Cardynham House**

Open All year

★★★★
🥾 **0.1mile(s) (0.1km)** ⌖ **SO868098**
*Mr John Paterson*
The Cross, Painswick, Glos, GL6 6XX
**T:** 01452 814006
**F:** 01452 812321
**E:** info@cardynham.co.uk
**W:** www.cardynham.co.uk
🛏 6 £69 🛏 3 £79

---

🚭 ♙ V 🌢 🗲     Mastercard, Visa, Amex, Delta
All rooms en-suite

---

B&B **Hale Cottage**

All year

🥾 **0.3mile(s) (0.5km)** ⌖ **SO867097**
*Mrs Lyn Thornton*
Hale Lane, Painswick, Glos, GL6 6QF
**T:** 01452 812992
**M:** 07759 591954
**E:** halecottage@btinternet.com
**W:** www.halecottage.com
🛏 3 £80
🚭 V DRY
All rooms en-suite

---

B&B **Hambutts Mynd**

All year

◆◆◆
🥾 **on Trail** ⌖ **SO865097**
*Mrs Elizabeth Warland*
Edge Road, Painswick, Glos, GL6 6UP
**T:** 01452 812352
**E:** ewarland@aol.com
🛏 1 £55 🛏 1 £55 🛏 1 £30
🚭 ♙ (Min 10 years)  V 🌢 DRY 🗆 🐾
All rooms en-suite

---

B&B **Meadowcote**

Closed Dec, Jan, Feb

◆◆◆◆
🥾 **on Trail** ⌖ **SO866096**
*Mrs Andrena Lock*
Stroud Road, Painswick, Glos, GL6 6UT

**T:** 01452 813565

2 £60  2 £35

Some rooms en-suite

**M** Pleasant, spacious house with parking, near centre of village. Excellent pubs/restaurants for evening meals nearby. Single occupancy of double rooms £45

## **B** Orchard House

**All year**

 **0.2mile(s) (0.25km)** SO866095

*Mrs Barbara Harley*

4 Court Orchard, Painswick, Glos, GL6 6UU

**T:** 01452 813150

**M:** 07887 892857

**F:** 01452 813150

**E:** harleydy@btinternet.com

1 £50  1 £60

Some rooms en-suite

## **B** St Annes

**Closed Christmas**

◆◆◆

**on Trail** SO867098

*Mrs Iris McCormick*

Gloucester Street, Painswick, Glos, GL6 6QN

**T:** 01452 812879

**M:** 07968 425128

**E:** greg-iris@supanet.com

**W:** www.st-annes-painswick.co.uk

1 £57  1 £57  1 £35

**M** The Green Tourism Business Scheme (Silver)

## **B&B** Thorne

**Closed Dec, Jan, Feb**

◆◆◆

 **0.1mile(s) (0.1km)** SO868098

*Mrs Barbara Blatchley*

Friday Street, Painswick, Glos, GL6 6QJ

**T:** 01452 812476

**F:** 01452 810925

1 £56  1 £56

**M** Single occupancy of rooms £30

## EDGE

**on Trail** SO850091

🍺 **The Edgemoor Inn**

**T:** 01452 813576

## **B&B** Gable End House

**Closed Christmas**

◆◆◆

 **0.9mile(s) (1.4km)** SO848079

*Mrs Lynne Partridge*

Pitchcombe, Nr Stroud, Glos, GL6 6LN

**T:** 01452 812166

**F:** 01452 812719

2 £50

All rooms en-suite

# 9 Painswick to Kings Stanley

 **The Withyholt**

*All year*

◆◆◆◆

 **0.6mile(s) (0.9km)** N SO848100

*Mrs Una Peacey*

Paul Mead, Edge, Nr Stroud,
Glos, GL6 6PG

**T:** 01452 813618

🛏 I £60 🛏 I £60 🛏 I £65 🛏 I £30
🚭 ✾ (Min 2 years) 🐾 📺 V 🐕 **DRY** 🔘 ▲
Some rooms en-suite

 **Upper Doreys Mill**

*All year*

◆◆◆

 **0.5mile(s) (0.8km)** N SO856098

*Mrs Sylvia Marden*

Edge, Nr Painswick, Glos, GL6 6NF

**T:** 01452 812459

**E:** sylvia@doreys.co.uk

**W:** www.doreys.co.uk

🛏 2 £60 🛏 I £60
🚭 ✾ V **DRY** 📷
💳 Mastercard, Visa, Delta
All rooms en-suite
🅗 Single occupancy of rooms £40

## HARESFIELD

 **Imile(s) (1.6 km)** N SO814100
🍺 **The Beacon Inn T:** 01452 728884
📞

 **The Beacon Inn**

*All year*

◆◆◆

 **0.7mile(s) (1.2km)** N SO813100

*Mr Terry Knight*

Haresfield, Stonehouse, Glos, GL10 3DX

**T:** 01452 728884

**E:** terry@thebeaconinn.co.uk

**W:** www.thebeaconinn.co.uk

🛏 2 £50 🛏 2 £60 🛏 I £45
🚭 V 🐕 🌜 🚗 ▲
💳 Mastercard, Visa, Delta
All rooms en-suite

## SHORTWOOD

 **on Trail** N SO832086
🅿 **Shortwood National Trust**
N SO832086

## RANDWICK

 **0.2mile(s) (0.35km)** N SO830068
🍺 **The Vine Tree Inn**
**T:** 01453 763748
📞
🅿 **Randwick Ash** N SO824066

## Court Farm

**Closed 23-26 Dec**

 **0.6mile(s) (1km)**  **SO827065**

*Mrs Diana Taylor*

Randwick, Stroud, Glos, GL6 6HH

**T:** 01453 764210

🛏 2 £56 🛏 1 £56 🛏 1 £75

🚫 ✸ 🏠 **V** 🏃 **DRY** 👣

All rooms en-suite

🍴 Court Farm is a 17th C farmhouse with original beams, panoramic views of the Stroud valley, large gardens with many interesting trees.

## Pretoria Villa

**Closed Christmas and New Year**

★★★★

 **7.5mile(s) (12km)** **SO891044**

*Mrs Glynis Solomon*

Wells Road, Eastcombe, Stroud Glos, GL6 7EE,

**T:** 01452 770435

**F:** 01452 770435

**E:** glynis@gsolomon.freeserve.co.uk

**W:** www.bedandbreakfast-cotswold.co.uk

🛏 1 £56 🛏 1 £56 🛏 1 £28

🚫 ✸ **V** 🏃 **DRY** 🚗 👣

## WESTRIP

 **0.3mile(s) (0.5km)** **SO826060**

🍺 **The Carpenter's Arms**

**T:** 01453 762693

📞 **TAXI**

## P by prior arrangement only, The Croft Farm Ebley **T:** 01453 764376

**SO824055**

## The Croft Farm

**Closed Nov - April**

 **0.2mile(s) (0.4km)** **SO824055**

*Mrs Julia Curry*

Foxmoor Lane, Ebley, Stroud, Glos, GL5 4PN

**T:** 01453 764376

**F:** 01453 764376

**M:** 07977 215715

**E:** thecroftfarmcampsite@fsmail.net

⛺ 4 £3

🏃 **DRY** 👥 🚰 🚰

🍴 All bookings by arrangement only. Packed lunches for campers and day walkers - local produce, mainly organic. Daily car parking available by arrangement £3 per day.

## STONEHOUSE

 **0.6mile(s) (1km)** **SO807052**

🏪 🧺 🎁 ✈ £ 📖 ✚ ✉ 👥 **TAXI** 🚌 🚂

# 10
*Section*

## Kings Stanley to Dursley

### 7.2 mile(s) (11.6 km)

From Kings Stanley, the Trail passes through the village of Middleyard before climbing up into Penn Wood. It is in Penn Wood that the two route options mentioned in section 9 converge again. The Cotswold Way takes you through the woods on the edge of the escarpment to emerge at Coaley Peak – a picnic area with magnificent views. The Trail then passes a disused quarry (the rock face clearly showing the structure of the underlying rock), before following another woodland path that eventually emerges in the valley with Cam Long Down ahead. The climb onto Cam Long Down is steep but the reward is lovely views across the Severn Vale, and back onto the escarpment because this is an outlier hill that has in the past broken away from the main escarpment. The Trail then goes down into the valley at Farfield passing through farmland into the market town of Dursley.

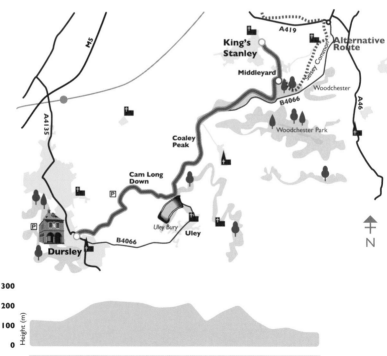

Kings Stanley to Dursley **7.2 mile(s) (11.6 km)**

## KINGS STANLEY

🛏 **0.15mile(s) (0.25km)** ⌖ **SO812035**
🍺 **The Kings Head T:**01453 825920
🧺 📞 ✉ **TAXI**
🚌
ℙ **High Street** ⌖ **SO811035**

### Court Farm

All year

🛏 **0.1mile(s) (0.2km)** ⌖ **SO812033**
*Mrs Fletcher*
Broad Street, King's Stanley, Glos, GL10 3PN
**T:** 01453 823127
⚑ 10 £3 ppn
👪 🕐 🚰 🚰

### Nurashell

All year

🛏 **0.2mile(s) (0.4km)** ⌖ **SO811034**
*Mrs Mavis Rollins*
Bath Road, King's Stanley, Glos, GL10 3JG
**T:** 01453 823642
🛏 1 £48 ⚑ 1 £48
🚫 👪 V 🏔 **DRY**
⛺ Member of the R.A. A walker with local
knowledge. Close to village shops and pub

### Orchardene

All year

🛏 **0.6mile(s) (0.9km)** ⌖ **SO810032**
*Ms Lesley Williams*
Castle Street, King's Stanley, Glos, GL10 3JX

**T:** 01453 822684
**F:** 01453 821554
**E:** toranda@btconnect.com
⚑ 2 £45
🚫 👪 (Min 10 years) ♿ 📷 V 🏔 🚭 **DRY**
🔲 🐾
⛺ All local and organic food - as far as possible!

### Stantone

All year

🛏 **0.4mile(s) (0.6km)** ⌖ **SO816030**
*Mrs Louise Walker*
Coldwell Lane, Middleyard, King's Stanley,
Glos, GL10 3PR
**T:** 01453 822204
**M:** 07963 353553
⚑ 1 £44
🚫 V 🏔 **DRY** 🔲 🚗 🐾 🖼
⛺ Free transport to pub for evening meal.
Peaceful location with wonderful views.
Warm welcome guaranteed.

# 10 Kings Stanley to Dursley

## B&B Valley Views

**All year**

★★★★
🛏 **on Trail** 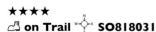 **SO818031**
*Mrs Pamela White*
12 Orchard Close, Middleyard, King's
Stanley, Stonehouse, Glos, GL10 3QA
**T:** 01453 827458
**M:** 07790 891128
**E:** enquiries@valley-views.com
**W:** www.valley-views.com
🛏 2 £56 🛏 1 £56
🚭 ⚲ (Min 6 years) 🕺 V 🔥 🌓 DRY 🔘 👣 📞
Some rooms en-suite
♨ Stunning views. Landscaped gardens with sun terrace. Guest's own sitting room. Extensive home-cooked evening menu.

## SUPERSTORE, DUDBRIDGE, STROUD

🛏 **0.1mile(s) (0.2 km)** **SO 834045**
🧺 🍴 🖥 👥

## SELSLEY

🛏 **0.1mile(s) (0.2 km)** **SO835039**
🍺 **The Bell Inn T:** 01453 764910
📞

## B&B Little Owl Cottage

**Closed Nov - Feb**

★★★★
🛏 **0.7mile(s) (1.2km)** **SO833034**
*Mrs Sara Elam*
Selsley Hill, Stroud, Glos, GL5 5LN
**T:** 01453 757050
**E:** littleowlcottage@btconnect.com
**W:** www.littleowlcottagebedandbreakfast.co.uk
🛏 1 £55 🛏 1 £55
🚭 ⚲ (Min 14 years) V 🔥 DRY 🚗 👣 📷
All rooms en-suite

## B&B The Yew Tree B & B

**closed Christmas and New Year**

◆◆◆◆ ★★★★
🛏 **2.1mile(s) (3.3km)** **SO866021**
*Mrs Elizabeth Peters*
Walls Quarry, Brimscombe, Stroud, Glos, GL5 2PA
**T:** 01453 887980
**F:** 01453 883428
**E:** info@theyewtreestroud.co.uk
**W:** www.theyewtree.absolutely-fabulous.net
🛏 1 £37 🛏 1 £60 🛏 1 £30
🚭 ⚲ 🕺 V DRY 🔘 📞 📷
♨ Holiday Cottage also available, sleeps 2-4 persons from £145 per week

## Nympsfield

🛏 **0.4mile (0.6km)** ⌖ **SO802004**
🍺 **The Rose & Crown**
**T:**01453 860240
📞

**Silver Street Farmhouse**
All year

◆◆◆◆
🛏 **0.9mile(s) (1.5km)** ⌖ **SO780012**
*Mrs N Dyer*
Coaley, Nr Dursley, Glos, GL11 5AX
**T:** 01453 860514
🛏 1 £55 🛏 2 £55
 🚭 V 🏔 DRY 🚗 🧗
Some rooms en-suite

## Uley

🛏 **0.4mile(s) (0.6km)** ⌖ **ST793986**
🍺 **The Old Crown Inn**
**T:**01453 860502
🧺 📞 ✉
🚌 No Sunday Service
Ⓟ **Uley Bury** ⌖ **ST786994**

**B&B** **Hodgecombe Farm**
⛺ Closed Nov - Mar

◆◆◆◆
🛏 **on Trail** ⌖ **ST783993**
*Mrs Catherine Bevan*
Cotswold Way, Uley, Glos, GL11 5AN
**T:** 01453 860365
**E:** hodgecombefarm@waitrose.com
**W:** www.hodgecombefarm.co.uk
🛏 1 £57 🛏 1 £57 ⛺ 5 £6
🚭 ⛹ (Min 5 years) V 🏔 🚫 🧗 🚶 ♿ 🦽 🚰
Some rooms en-suite
⛺ Camping closed mid Sept to Easter.
Directly on the Cotswold Way with
stunning views over the Severn Vale. All
rooms have coffee/tea facilities, armchair
and welcoming extras.

# 11
## *Section*

## Dursley to Wotton Under Edge
### 7.3 mile(s) (11.8km)

Leaving Dursley, the Cotswold Way climbs steeply up onto Stinchcombe Hill, where those who wish to enjoy the magnificent views can walk the full distance around the perimeter of the hill. Alternatively, you can take the shortcut directly across the neck of the hill from the golf club. The Trail descends through woodland into farmland and follows a track into the village of North Nibley. From North Nibley there is another steep ascent to the Tyndale Monument before the Trail levels out across the grassland and through woodland leading onto Wotton Hill, with its curious walled enclosure of trees that were first planted in 1815 to commemorate the battle of Waterloo. The Trail then descends into the town of Wotton under Edge.

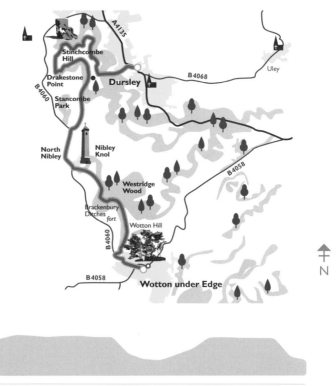

Dursley to Wotton under Edge **7.3 mile(s) (11.8 km)**

## DURSLEY

 **on Trail** <sup>w</sup>✛<sup>E</sup> **ST756982**

🏨🛒🚌🍵🛍️£🏠➕🔌✉️👤 **TAXI**

🚌 No Sunday Service

Ⓟ **Castle Street Long Stay**

✛ **ST756984**

---

### B | 11 Shakespeare Road

**Closed end Oct to Easter**

 **0.4mile(s) (0.6km)** <sup>w</sup>✛<sup>E</sup> **ST763974**

*Mrs Veronica Harding*

Dursley, Glos, GL11 4QE

**T:** 01453 547080

**E:** ronnieh@onetel.com

🛏️ 1 £40 🛏️ 1 £20

⊗ V 🐾 **DRY** 🔲 🖼️

---

### B | 7 Prospect Place

**All year**

 **on Trail** ✛ **ST755981**

*Mrs Cecilia Boyle*

7 Prospect Place, May Lane, Dursley, Glos, GL11 4JL

**T:** 01453 543445

**M:** 07960 285533

**E:** ceciliaboyle@hotmail.com

**W:** www.dursleybedandbreakfast.co.uk

🛏️ 1 £52 🛏️ 1 £52 🛏️ 2 £26

⊗ 👫 (Min 3 years) 🐱 V 🐾 **DRY** 🔲

🔔 Prospect Place is a listed building

---

### B&B  Foresters

**All year**

◆◆◆◆

 **1mile(s) (1.6km)** <sup>w</sup>✛<sup>E</sup> **SO750002**

*Mrs Victoria Jennings*

31 Chapel Street, Cam, Dursley, Glos, GL11 5NX

**T:** 01453 549996

**M:** 07973 890477

**F:** 01453 549996

**E:** foresters@freeuk.com

🛏️ 2 £58 🛏️ 2 £58 🛏️ 2 £POA 🛏️ 1 £36

⊗ 👫 🐱 V 🐾 **DRY** 🔲 🔔 🖼️

---

### B&B The Garden Flat

**Closed 23 Dec - 2 Jan**

 **0.1mile(s) (0.2km)** <sup>w</sup>✛<sup>E</sup> **ST759980**

*Mrs Louisa Rubin*

Ormond House, 13 Bull Pitch, Dursley, Glos, GL11 4NG

**T:** 01453 545312

🛏️ 1 £28

⊗ 👫 V 🐾 👣

All rooms en-suite

🔔 The Garden Flat is an annexe to our grade II listed Georgian town house. It is a self-contained flat with fully fitted kitchen, twin bedroom and en-suite bathroom. Bookings taken for longer self-catering holidays.

# 11 Dursley to Wotton Under Edge

## NORTH NIBLEY

🥾 **on Trail** ᴺ⌖ᴱ **ST740957**
🍺 **The Black Horse Inn**
**T:** 01453 543777
🧺 **☎**
🚌 No weekend service
P **Lower House Lane** ⌖ **ST738962**
**H Parking only available for 3 cars**

### 🅸🅽🅽 Black Horse Inn
**B&B** All year

🥾 **on Trail** ᴺ⌖ᴱ **ST740958**
*Mrs Candice Nabb*
I Barrs Lane, North Nibley, Glos,
GL11 6DT
**T:** 01453 543777
**F:** 01453 545526
**E:** nabbblkhrs@tiscali.co.uk
🛏 6 £65 🛏 I £95
⚒ V 🚿 🌑 DRY ☎
🏧 Mastercard, Visa, Amex
All rooms en-suite

### B&B Burrows Court
Dec - Jan

★★★
🥾 **0.5mile(s) (0.8km)** ᴺ⌖ᴱ **ST731967**
*Mr Peter Rackley*
Nibley Green, North Nibley, Dursley,
GL11 6AZ, Glos
**T:** 01453 546230
**F:** 01453 546230
**E:** burrowscourt@tesco.net
**W:** www.burrowscourt.co.uk
🛏 3 £52 🛏 2 £52 🛏 I £67
🚫 ⚒ 📶 V 🚿 DRY 📷 🎿
🏧 Mastercard, Visa, Amex, Delta (+4%)
All rooms en-suite
**H See website**

### B&B Innocks House
All year

🥾 **on Trail** ᴺ⌖ᴱ **ST740958**
*Mrs Kirsten Marlow*
North Nibley, Dursley, Glos, GL11 6DR
**T:** 01453 546754
**M:** 07850 014382
**E:** bill-kirsten.marlow@tesco.net
🛏 2 £55
⚒ V 🚿 DRY ☎ 🎿
All rooms en-suite
**H Single occupancy of rooms £30**

# Dursley to Wotton Under Edge

 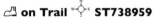 **Nibley House**

**All year**

👢 **on Trail** ✛ **ST738959**

*Mrs Diana Eley*

North Nibley, Dursley, Glos, GL11 6DL

**T:** 01453 543108

**F:** 01453 544104

**E:** john@eley7143.freeserve.co.uk

**W:** www.nibleyhouse.co.uk

🛏 2 £30 🛏 2 £30 🛏 1 £30 🛏 2 £30

⚠ 6 £4 ppn 🚐 5 £5 ppn

🚫 📷 V 🔥 **DRY** 🔘 🚗 📠 📖 🚹 🚿 🚽

💳 Mastercard, Visa, Amex, Delta, Switch, Solo, Electra, JCB

All rooms en-suite

# 12
## *Section*

The Cotswold Way follows a stream out of Wotton under Edge, before climbing back up onto the escarpment, passing close to the National Trust property of Newark Park. The Trail then makes for the village of Alderley down a glorious sunken woodland track. From Alderley the route passes through a peaceful valley where you can see remains of Medieval ridge and furrow either side when the light is right. On reaching Lower Kilcott a clear millstream runs alongside the quiet road that the Cotswold Way follows. The route then climbs gently up to the Somerset Monument before heading towards the village of Hawkesbury Upton.

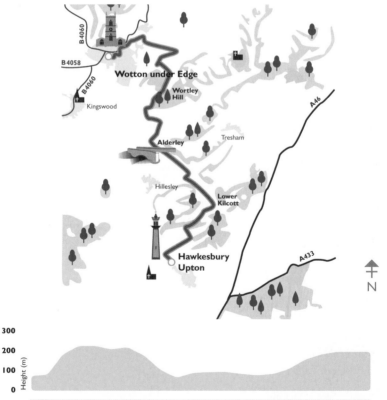

Wotton under Edge to Hawkesbury **7.4 mile(s) (11.9 km)**

## WOTTON UNDER EDGE

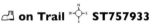 **on Trail**  **ST757933**

🏠🛒🍽🏧£🖼➕📞✉🏃 **TAXI**

🚌 No Sunday service

P **Potters Pond** ⊹ **ST759934**

### B | New House

**Closed 25-26 Dec**

👢 **1mile(s) (1.6km)** ⊹ **ST753903**

*Jean Simmons*

Folly Farm, Kingswood, Wotton-Under-
Edge, Glos, GL12 7QX

**T:** 01453 842110

**M:** 07748 484942

**F:** 01453 842110

🛏 1 £50 🛏 2 £50 🛏 2 £25

🚭 🏃 (Min 12 years) 📷 V 🏔 🌙 DRY 🍳

Some rooms en-suite

### B | The Ridings

**Closed Dec and Jan**

👢 **0.6mile(s) (1km)** ⊹ **ST769952**

*Mrs Janet Poole*

Bowcott, Wotton-Under-Edge, Glos, GL12 7PT

**T:** 01453 842128

**E:** j.poole1@homecall.co.uk

🛏 2 £50 🛏 1 £50

🚭 🏃 📷 V 🏔 🌙 DRY 🍳 🚗 🚶

### B&B | Wotton Guest House

**All year**

👢 **on Trail** ⊹ **ST756933**

*Mrs Sandra Nixon*

31a Long Street, Wotton-Under-Edge, Glos, GL12 7BX

**T:** 01453 843158

**E:** wottongh@aol.com

**W:** www.smoothound.co.uk

🛏 3 £55 🛏 2 £55 🛏 1 £60 🛏 1 £35

🏃 V DRY 🐕 📞

VISA Mastercard, Visa, Amex

All rooms en-suite

🏠 17th century cotswold manor house in
walled garden, carpark to rear.

## HILLESLEY

👢 **0.6mile(s) (1km)** ⊹ **ST769897**

🍺 **The Fleece Inn T:**01453 843189

📞

🚌 No Sunday service

# 12 Wotton Under Edge to Hawkesbury

## B&B Bridge Farmhouse

All year

🥾 **on Trail** ⊹ **ST787892**

*Mrs Wendy Watchman*

Lower Kilcott, Wotton-Under-Edge, Glos, GL12 7RL

**T:** 01454 238254

**E:** bridgefarm@tiscali.co.uk

🛏 2 £50 🛏 1 £50

🚭 👯 V 🔥 🄰 **DRY** 🔟 📐 📞 🖼

Some rooms en-suite

ℍ 16th C farmhouse with ford and stream. Extensive gardens

## B&B Half Acre Cottage

All year

🥾 **0.5mile(s) (0.8km)** ⊹ **ST767897**

*Mrs Jane Kendall*

Kingswood Rd, Hillesley, Wotton-Under-Edge, Glos, GL12 7RB

**T:** 01453 844619

**E:** janekendall@onetel.com

🛏 1 £50 🛏 2 £25

ℍ A pretty cottage with friendly service.

## B&B Hillesley Mill

Closed Christmas

◆◆◆

🥾 **0.2mile(s) (0.4km)** ⊹ **ST770905**

*Mrs Julie James*

Alderley, Wotton-Under-Edge, Glos, GL12 7QT

**T:** 01453 843258

**M:** 07867 687078

🛏 1 £50 🛏 1 £55

👯 📷 V 🔥 **DRY** 🔟 🚗 📐

Some rooms en-suite

ℍ Electric blanket, tea & coffee making facilities

## B&B The Old Farmhouse

All year

🥾 **on Trail** ⊹ **ST769909**

*Mrs S Shearer*

Alderley, Wotton-Under-Edge, Glos, GL12 7QT

**T:** 01453 843454

**E:** sophiecharles@tiscali.co.uk

**W:** www.sophiecharles.com

🛏 1 £70 🛏 2 £50 🛏 2 £70

👯 V 🔥 **DRY** 🔟 🖼

ℍ Cost of single occupancy £45. Rates may vary - please confirm when booking

# Section

## Hawkesbury to Tormarton

### 7.7 mile(s) (12.4 km)

Passing an ancient drovers pond, the Cotswold Way follows Bath Lane south towards Horton. Before reaching the National Trust property of Horton Court (probably the oldest vicarage in England with a fine Tudor Hall) the Trail climbs up onto Horton Fort, with extensive views opening out over the Severn Vale and beyond. The Trail then crosses farmland, to the villages of Horton and then Old Sodbury. From here the Trail passes through the magnificent Capability Brown Parkland of Dodington Park before crossing the final few fields into the village of Tormarton.

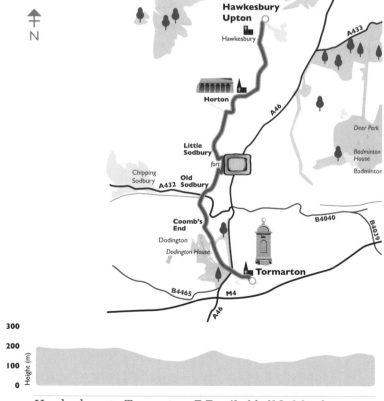

Hawkesbury to Tormarton **7.7 mile(s) (12.4 km)**

# 13   Hawkesbury to Tormaton

## HAWKESBURY UPTON

👢 **0.2mile(s) (0.3km)** ⊹ **ST780869**
🍺 **The Beaufort Arms T:**01454 238217
🍺 **The Fox Inn T:**01454 238219
🧺 📞 ✉ **TAXI**
🚌   No Sunday Service
🅿 **Please park considerately here as there is no officially designated parking available**

### B&B   Coombe Farm

**All year**

👢 **0.1mile(s) (0.1km)** ⊹ **ST778873**
*Mrs Audrey Cole*
Hawkesbury Upton, Badminton, South Glos, GL9 1AY
**T:**01454 238202
🛏 3 £24 🛏 1 £POA
🧑‍🤝‍🧑 ♿ V 🔲 🐾

### B&B   New Crosshands Farm

**All year**

👢 **on Trail** ⊹ **ST761826**
*Mrs Deborah Snell*
Little Sodbury, Little Sodbury, South Glos, BS37 6RJ
**T:**01454 316366
🛏 2 £60 🛏 1 £60 🛏 1 £60
🚫 🧑‍🤝‍🧑 (Min 6 months) V 🐾 🌳
Some rooms en-suite
🅿 Cotswold Stone farm house located on the Cotswold Way

## INN   The Fox Inn

**Closed 25 & 26 December**

👢 **0.2mile(s) (0.4km)** ⊹ **ST778869**
*Mrs Ann Arney*
High Street, Hawkesbury Upton, South Glos, GL9 1AU
**T:**01454 238219
🛏 2 £55 🛏 2 £55 🛏 1 £POA
🧑‍🤝‍🧑 🐾 V 🐾 🌳 👶 🖼
💳 Mastercard, Visa, Delta
All rooms en-suite

## OLD SODBURY

👢 **on Trail** ⊹ **ST752826**
🍺 **The Dog Inn T:**01454 312006
🧺 📞 ✉ **TAXI**
🚌   No Sunday Service

### B&B   Denison Cottage

**Closed Nov to Feb**

👢 **on Trail** ⊹ **ST754806**
*Mrs Susan Holbrook*
Combs End, Old Sodbury, Bristol, BS37 6SQ
**T:**01454 311510
🛏 1 £55
🚫 🧑‍🤝‍🧑 (Min 5 years) 🐾 V 🐾 DRY 🔲 👶
📞 🖼
🅿 Scandinavian cabin situated in beautiful 2 acre garden in an area of outstanding natural beauty

##  Dog Inn & Cottages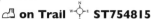

**All year**

🥾 **on Trail** ⌖ **ST754815**

*Miss Nicki Harris*

Badminton Road, Old Sodbury, South Glos, BS37 6LZ

**T:** 01454 312006

🛏 10 £50 🛏 6 £50 🛏 2 £70 🛏 2 £30

⊘ 🍴 ♿ 🔲 V 🜂 🜨 DRY 🔲 👫 📞 🖼

Mastercard, Visa, Delta

Some rooms en-suite

## Kingrove Farm

**All year**

🥾 **3mile(s) (4.8km)** ⌖ **ST732813**

*Mr Colin Watson*

Chipping Sodbury, Bristol, BS37 6DY,

**T:** 01454 312314

🛏 2 £50 🛏 1 £50 🛏 2 £25

⊘ 🍴 🔲 DRY 🚗 🖼

Some rooms en-suite

## Sodbury House Hotel

**All year**

◆◆◆◆

🥾 **0.2mile(s) (0.3km)** ⌖ **ST751816**

*Mr Guy Gardner*

Old Sodbury, South Glos, BS37 6LU

**T:** 01454 312847

**M:** 07765 886281

**F:** 01454 237105

**E:** sodburyhouse.hotel@virgin.net

**W:** www.sodburyhouse.co.uk

🛏 5 £70 🛏 4 £70 🛏 6 £50

⊘ 🍴 ♿ V 🜂 DRY 👫

Mastercard, Visa, Delta

All rooms en-suite

🍴 Very good pub food within 300m

## B&B The Moda Hotel

**All year**

◆◆◆◆

🥾 **1.2mile(s) (2km)** ⌖ **ST726822**

*Mrs Joanna Macarthur*

1 High St, Chipping Sodbury, South Glos, BS37 6BA

**T:** 01454 312135

**F:** 01454 850090

**E:** enquiries@modahotel.com

**W:** www.modahotel.com

🛏 4 £78 🛏 1 £78 🛏 1 £98 🛏 4 £62

⊘ 🍴 🔲 V DRY 🔲

Mastercard, Visa, Delta

All rooms en-suite

# 14
*Section*

## Tormarton to Cold Ashton

### 6.6 mile(s) (10.6 km)

The Trail leaves Tormarton to the south along the Marshfield Road, then crosses arable land that eventually leads to a path passing round the perimeter wall of Dyrham Park – a William and Mary mansion nestling in an ancient deer park. Access to this National Trust property can be gained from the village of Dyrham – the next destination. From here the Trail climbs up into Dyrham Woods before continuing through farmland into the village of Cold Ashton, with its magnificent rectory and manor house (both in private ownership).

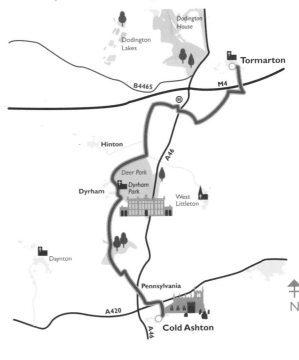

Tormarton to Cold Ashton **6.6 mile(s) (10.6km)**

## TORMARTON VILLAGE

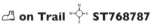

🥾 **on Trail** <sup>N</sup>◈<sup>E</sup> **ST768787**

🍺 **The Compass Inn T:**01454 218242

🍺 **The Portcullis Inn T:**01454 218263

🚌 No Sunday Service except National Trust bus (seasonal)

P **Picnic Area M4/A46 interchange**
◈ **ST756777**

### 🅱 Chestnut Farm

**All year**

🥾 **0.1mile(s) (0.1km)** <sup>N</sup>◈<sup>E</sup> **ST768790**

*R Cadei*

Tormarton, Nr Badminton, South Glos, GL9 1HS

**T:** 01454 218563

**W:** www.chestnut-farm.co.uk

🛏 5 £70 🛏 2 £60

🚫 ✝ 🖳 V 🔥 🜚 DRY 🚗 👣 🗺

### 🅱 Noades House

**Closed Nov - Feb**

🥾 **0.1mile(s) (0.2km)** <sup>N</sup>◈<sup>E</sup> **ST765788**

*Mrs Jane Smart*

Tormarton, South Glos, GL9 1JA

**T:** 01454 218746

🛏 1 £45 🛏 1 £25 🏕 3 £5

🚫 ✝ (Min 5 years) V 🔥 DRY 👣 🜚 🚰 🗺

### B&B Old Hundred Coach House

**All year**

🥾 **0.1mile(s) (0.2km)** <sup>N</sup>◈<sup>E</sup> **ST765788**

*Mrs Deirdra Baker*

Old Hundred Lane, Tormarton,
South Glos, GL9 1JA

**T:** 01454 218420

**E:** deedaveb@yahoo.co.uk

🛏 1 £50

🚫 ✝ 🖳 V 🔥 DRY 🜚 🚗 👣

### ⓗ The Compass Inn

🏕 **Closed Christmas and New Year**

★★

🥾 **0.2mile(s) (0.4km)** <sup>N</sup>◈<sup>E</sup> **ST765785**

*Mr Paul Monyard*

Tormarton, Nr Badminton, South Glos GL9 1JB,

**T:** 01454 218242

**F:** 01454 218741

**E:** info@compass-inn.co.uk

**W:** www.compass-inn.co.uk

🛏 12 £80 🛏 7 £70 🛏 6 £80

🛏 1 £70 🏕 Field £POA

✝ ♿ 🖳 V 🔥 🜚 DRY 🜚 🚗 🜚 ♿WC 🚰

💳 Mastercard, Visa, Amex, Delta, Diners

All rooms en-suite

🗏 Smoking restriction in some areas.

Camping in field at discretion of manager.

## TORMARTON PICNIC AREA

🛏 **on Trail** ⊕ **ST755776**
🏠 📞 ⊛
🅿 **Picnic Area M4/A46 interchange**
⊕ **ST756777**

## A46 / TOLLDOWN FARM
### CROSS ROADS

🛏 **0.4mile(s) (0.6km)** ⊕ **ST753769**
🍺 **The Crown T:**01225 891166

## HINTON

🛏 **0.7mile(s) (1.2km)** ⊕ **ST734768**
🍺 **The Bull T:**0117 937 2332
⊠ 📞

## DYRHAM

🛏 **on Trail** ⊕ **ST740757**
🫖 (Dyrham Park) 📞
🚌 National Trust bus (seasonal)

## PENNSYLVANIA

🛏 **on Trail** ⊕ **ST744733**
⊛

### B&B Old Swan Cottage
*All year*

🛏 **on Trail** ⊕ **ST744733**
*Mrs Angela Mutlow*
Pennsylvania, Near Chippenham, SN14 8LB
**T:** 01225 891419
**M:** 07884 495145
**E:** angie@old-swan-cottage.co.uk
**W:** www.old-swan-cottage.co.uk
🛏 1 £60 🛏 2 £60 🛏 1 £70 🛏 1 £35
👫 (Min 10 years) **V** 🔥 **DRY** 🔲
All rooms en-suite

# Section

## Cold Ashton to Bath

### 10.2 mile(s) (16.5 km)

The Cotswold Way leaves Cold Ashton and descends into the beautiful secluded valley at Lower Hamswell. The next climb takes you up to the site where the bloody civil war battle of Lansdown was fought. From here the Trail levels out across the plateau, passing the promontory hill fort at Little Down and the famous Bath race course. The path emerges at Prospect Stile and it is from here that the first glimpse of the City of Bath is viewed in the valley below. The Trail then descends along a broad track and through farmland to arrive at Weston outside Bath. From here the Trail changes in character, becoming more urban as you begin your journey into Bath – the only entire city in the United Kingdom to be given world heritage status. The Cotswold Way gives you glimpses of the fine parks and regency architecture for which the city is famous on its way to the final destination of Bath Abbey.

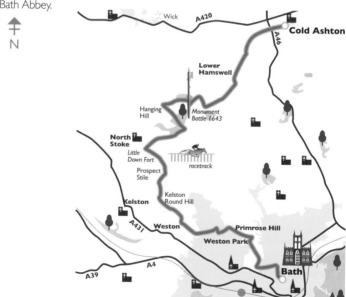

Cold Ashton to Bath **10.2 mile(s) (16.5 km)**

# 15 Cold Ashton to Bath

## COLD ASHTON

🛏 **on Trail** ⌖ **749726**
🍺 **The White Hart T:**01225 891233
📞 **TAXI**
🚌 No Sunday Service
Ⓟ **Parish Hall** ⌖ **ST747726**

## B&B Knowle Hill Farm

All year

🛏 **2mile(s) (3.2km)** ⌖ **ST825729**
*Mrs Cynthia Bond*
Beeks Lane, Marshfield, Chippenham, Wilts,
SN14 8BB
**T:** 01225 891503
**E:** cynthia_bond@hotmail.co.uk
🛏 1 £25 🛏 1 £POA 🛏 1 £POA
⚥ 📷 V 🏔 DRY

## B&B The Chestnuts

⛺ June to October

🛏 **on Trail** ⌖ **ST748725**
*Mr Dave Watts*
Cold Ashton, Chippenham, Wiltshire,
SN14 8JT
**T:** 01225 892020
**M:** 07711 050514
**F:** 01225 892054
**E:** thechestnuts@copperstream.co.uk
**W:** www.thechestnuts.info/chestnuts/Main/Home.htm
🛏 1 £60 🛏 1 £60 ⛺ 5 £4 🚐 2 £6
🚭 ⚥ ⚥ 📷 V 🏔 DRY 🐕 ⚥ ♿ ♿
All rooms en-suite

## B&B Toghill House Farm

All year

★★★★
🛏 **1mile(s) (1.6km)** ⌖ **ST731724**
*Mrs Jackie Bishop*
Freezinghill, Cold Ashton, Bristol, BS30 5RT,
**T:** 01225 891261
**F:** 01225 892128
**E:** accommodation@toghillhousefarm.co.uk
**W:** www.toghillhousefarm.co.uk
🛏 5 £68 🛏 3 £68 🛏 3 £85
🚭 ⚥ 📷 V 🏔 DRY 🔘 📞 ♿
💳 Mastercard, Visa, Delta
All rooms en-suite

## WESTON, BATH

🛏 **on Trail** ⌖ **ST728664**
🍺 **Kings Head T:**01255 310443
🍺 **Crown & Anchor T:**01255 421633
📞 ⚥ ✚

## BATH

🛏 **on Trail** ⌖ **ST750647**
🍺 🍴 🏨 🍵 🎬 £ 🖼 ✚ ✉ ⚥ 📞 TAXI
🚌 🚂

Ⓟ **numerous - follow signage**

**Athole Guest House**

All year

◆◆◆◆◆

🛏 **0.3mile(s) (0.5km)** ⊕ **ST742640**

*Dr Wolfgang Herrlinger*

33 Upper Oldfield Park, Bath, BA2 3JX,

**T:** 01225 320000

**F:** 01225 320009

**E:** info@atholehouse.co.uk

**W:** www.atholehouse.co.uk

🛏 4 £62 🛏 1 £72 🛏 2 £82 🛏 2 £52

🚭 ♔ ♕ V ♨ **DRY** 🔟 🚗 🐾 📞 📶

**VISA** Mastercard, Visa, Amex, Delta

All rooms en-suite

**Bath YMCA**

All Year

🛏 **0.1mile(s) (0.1km)** ⊕ **ST750651**

*The Manager*

International House, Broad Street Place,

Bath, BA1 5LH,

**T:** 01225 325900

**E:** stay@bathymca.co.uk

**W:** www.bathymca.co.uk

🛏 38 £36 🛏 3 £60 🛏 28 £24

🚭 ♔ 🔟

**VISA** Mastercard, Visa

 **Belmont Hotel**

Closed Christmas and New Year

★★★

🛏 **0.1mile(s) (0.2km)** ⊕ **ST749653**

*Mr Archie Watson*

7 Belmont, Lansdown Road, Bath, BA1 5DZ

**T:** 01225 423082

**M:** 07980 954789

**E:** archie_watson@hotmail.com

**W:** www.belmontbath.co.uk

🛏 4 £65 🛏 2 £65 🛏 1 £80 🛏 1 £40

🚭 ♔ V

Some rooms en-suite

**B&B** **Cranleigh**

Closed 25 & 26 December

◆◆◆◆

🛏 **0.5mile(s) (0.8km)** ⊕ **ST724655**

*Mrs Denise Potter*

159 Newbridge Hill, Bath, BA1 3PX,

**T:** 01225 310197

**F:** 01225 423143

**E:** cranleigh@btinternet.com

**W:** www.cranleighguesthouse.com

🛏 3 £60 🛏 2 £65 🛏 2 £85 🛏 1 £40

🚭 ♔ (Min 5 years) ♿ ♕ V **DRY** 🔟 📞

**VISA** Mastercard, Visa, Delta

All rooms en-suite

**B&B** **Devonshire House**

All year

◆◆◆◆

🛏 **1.3mile(s) (0.8km)** ⊕ **ST746631**

*Mrs Louise Fry*

143 Wellsway, Bath, BA2 4RZ,

**T:** 01225 312495

**E:** enquiries@devonshire-house.uk.com

**W:** www.devonshire-house.uk.com

🛏 4 £68 🛏 2 £68 🛏 1 £98

🚭 ♔ V ♨ **DRY** 🔟 📞

**VISA** Mastercard, Visa, Delta

All rooms en-suite

🛏 Self catering cottage also available.

Enquire about Spa Breaks

# 15 Cold Ashton to Bath

## H Haringtons Hotel

All year

★★

🥾 on Trail ⌖ ST749649

*Miss Melissa Pritchard*
8-10 Queen Street, Bath, BA1 1HE,
**T:** 01225 461728
**F:** 01225 444804
**E:** post@haringtonshotel.co.uk
**W:** www.haringtonshotel.co.uk
🛏 6 £88  4 £108  3 £118
🚭 ✸ V 🏔 ⓞ DRY ⓞ ⒣ ☎
VISA Mastercard, Visa, Amex, Delta
All rooms en-suite

## B&B Marlborough House

Closed 24 & 25 December

◆◆◆◆

🥾 0.1mile(s) (0.1km) ⌖ ST742651

*Mr Peter Richard*
1 Marlborough Lane, Bath, BA1 2NQ,
**T:** 01225 318175
**M:** 07960 907541
**F:** 01225 466127
**E:** mars@manque.dircon.co.uk
**W:** www.marlborough-house.net
🛏 4 £70  2 £70  2 £70
🚭 ✸ 🔌 V DRY ☎
VISA Mastercard, Visa, Delta
All rooms en-suite

## Å Newton Mill Caravan & Camping

All year

★★

🥾 1.6mile(s) (2.5km) ⌖ ST716648

*Mr Keith Davies*
Newton Road,
Bath, BA2 9JF,
**T:** 01225 333909
**F:** 01225 461556
**E:** newtonmill@hotmail.com
**W:** www.campinginbath.co.uk
Å 105 £7  90 £19.50
✸ 🔌 DRY ⓞ 🎮 ☎ ⓞ ♿ 🚿 🚰 📷 CG
VISA Visa, Delta
🏕 David Bellamy Conservation Award. Old Mill bar and restaurant. Frequent bus service to Bath and Bristol

## B&B Number 30

All year

◆◆◆◆

🥾 0.6mile(s) (1km) ⌖ ST744650

*Mr David Greenwood*
30 Crescent Gardens, Bath, BA1 2NB,
**T:** 01225 337393
**F:** 01225 337393
**E:** david.greenwood12@btinternet.com
**W:** www.numberthirty.com
🛏 3 £69  1 £80  1 £55
🚭 ✸ (Min 12 years) V DRY
VISA Mastercard, Visa
Some rooms en-suite
🏕 Located within 0.5 m of Bath city centre, Bath Spa and coach station within 15 minutes walk.

## B Radnor Guest House

**Closed Christmas**

★★★★

🛏 **0.6mile(s) (1km)** ⌖ **ST756645**

*Mrs Jane Briggs*

9 Pulteney Terrace, Bath, BA2 4HJ,

**T:** 01225 316159

**F:** 01225 319199

**E:** info@radnorguesthouse.co.uk

**W:** www.radnorguesthouse.co.uk

🛏 2 £52 🛏 1 £52 🛏 1 £65

🚭 ⚦ ♚ V DRY ☎

All rooms en-suite

⚑ Ground floor rooms available. Colour TV / radio alarm clocks / hair driers / tea and coffee making facilities in all rooms. Cost of single occupancy £40

## St Christophers

**All year**

🛏 **0.1mile(s) (0.2km)** ⌖ **ST750649**

*Mr Duane Vanner*

9 Green Street, Bath, BA1 2JY,

**T:** 01225 481444

**W:** www.st-christophers.co.uk

🛏 1 £24 Bunks 56 £13

V ▣

▨ Mastercard, Visa

⚑ Youth hostel, breakfast included. 20% discount at bar on most food and drink, late night bar showing most sporting events, located in central Bath

## ▲ YHA Bath

**All year**

★★★

🛏 **1.2mile(s) (2km)** ⌖ **ST766644**

*The Hostel Manager*

Bathwick Hill,

Bath, BA2 6JZ,

**T:** 0870 770 568

**E:** bath@yha.org.uk

**W:** www.yha.org.uk

🛏 5 £32 🛏 12 £54

🚭 ⚦ (Min 4 years) ♚ V ▨ ▣ DRY ▣ ☎

▨ Mastercard, Visa, Delta, Maestro

⚑ YHA is a membersip organisation, non members pay a £3 pppn supplement. Membership can be purchased on line or at any hostel. The hostel has a bar

# Distances between places along the Cotswold Way National Trail in miles

The chart below shows distances (in miles) between places along the Cotswold Way from Chipping Campden to Bath. There are two points on the Cotswold Way where there is a choice of route on the ground. This chart only takes one of those routes in both cases as follows:

*Painswick to Kings Stanley (via Kings Stanley & Middleyard - not over Selsley Common)*
*Kings Stanley to Dursley (via Kings Stanley & Middleyard - not over Selsley Common)*
*Dursley to Wotton under Edge (via long route around Stinchcombe Hill - not the short cut)*

| | Chipping Campden | Broadway | Wood Stanway | Winchcombe | Cleeve Hill | Dowdeswell | Leckhampton Hill | Birdlip | Painswick | Kings Stanley | Dursley | Wotton under Edge | Hawkesbury | Tormarton | Cold Ashton |
|---|---|---|---|---|---|---|---|---|---|---|---|---|---|---|---|
| Broadway | 6.0 | | | | | | | | | | | | | | |
| Wood Stanway | 12.5 | 6.5 | | | | | | | | | | | | | |
| Winchcombe | 17.9 | 12.0 | 5.4 | | | | | | | | | | | | |
| Cleeve Hill | 23.5 | 17.6 | 11.1 | 5.6 | | | | | | | | | | | |
| Dowdeswell | 29.1 | 23.1 | 16.6 | 11.1 | 5.5 | | | | | | | | | | |
| Leckhampton Hill | 33.8 | 27.8 | 21.4 | 15.8 | 10.2 | 4.7 | | | | | | | | | |
| Birdlip | 39.4 | 33.4 | 26.9 | 21.4 | 15.8 | 10.3 | 5.6 | | | | | | | | |
| Painswick | 48.0 | 42.0 | 35.5 | 30.1 | 24.5 | 18.9 | 14.2 | 8.6 | | | | | | | |
| Kings Stanley | 55.8 | 49.9 | 43.3 | 37.9 | 32.3 | 26.7 | 22.0 | 16.5 | 7.8 | | | | | | |
| Dursley | 63.0 | 57.0 | 50.5 | 45.1 | 39.4 | 33.9 | 29.2 | 23.6 | 15.0 | 7.2 | | | | | |
| Wotton under Edge | 70.3 | 64.3 | 57.8 | 52.3 | 46.7 | 41.2 | 36.5 | 30.9 | 22.3 | 14.5 | 7.3 | | | | |
| Hawkesbury | 77.7 | 71.7 | 65.2 | 59.7 | 54.1 | 48.6 | 43.9 | 38.3 | 29.7 | 21.8 | 14.7 | 7.4 | | | |
| Tormarton | 85.4 | 79.4 | 72.9 | 67.4 | 61.8 | 56.3 | 51.6 | 46.0 | 37.4 | 29.5 | 22.4 | 15.1 | 7.7 | | |
| Cold Ashton | 91.9 | 86.0 | 79.5 | 74.0 | 68.4 | 62.9 | 58.2 | 52.6 | 43.9 | 36.1 | 29.0 | 21.7 | 14.3 | 6.6 | |
| Bath | 102.2 | 96.2 | 89.7 | 84.2 | 78.6 | 73.1 | 68.4 | 62.8 | 54.2 | 46.4 | 39.2 | 31.9 | 24.5 | 16.8 | 10.2 |

# Distances between places along the Cotswold Way National Trail in kilometres

The chart below shows distances (in kilometres) between places along the Cotswold Way from Chipping Campden to Bath. There are two points on the Cotswold Way where there is a choice of route on the ground. This chart only takes one of those routes in both cases as follows:

*Painswick to Kings Stanley (via Kings Stanley & Middleyard – not over Selsley Common)*
*Kings Stanley to Dursley (via Kings Stanley & Middleyard – not over Selsley Common)*
*Dursley to Wotton under Edge (via long route around Stinchcombe Hill – not the short cut)*

| | Chipping Campden | Broadway | Wood Stanway | Winchcombe | Cleeve Hill | Dowdeswell | Leckhampton Hill | Birdlip | Painswick | Kings Stanley | Dursley | Wotton under Edge | Hawkesbury | Tormarton | Cold Ashton |
|---|---|---|---|---|---|---|---|---|---|---|---|---|---|---|---|
| Broadway | 9.6 | | | | | | | | | | | | | | |
| Wood Stanway | 20.1 | 10.5 | | | | | | | | | | | | | |
| Winchcombe | 28.9 | 19.3 | 8.8 | | | | | | | | | | | | |
| Cleeve Hill | 37.9 | 28.3 | 17.8 | 9.0 | | | | | | | | | | | |
| Dowdeswell | 46.8 | 37.2 | 26.7 | 17.9 | 8.9 | | | | | | | | | | |
| Leckhampton Hill | 54.4 | 44.8 | 34.3 | 25.5 | 16.5 | 7.6 | | | | | | | | | |
| Birdlip | 63.4 | 53.8 | 43.3 | 34.5 | 25.5 | 16.6 | 9.0 | | | | | | | | |
| Painswick | 77.3 | 67.7 | 57.2 | 48.4 | 39.4 | 30.5 | 22.9 | 13.9 | | | | | | | |
| Kings Stanley | 89.9 | 80.3 | 69.8 | 61.0 | 52.0 | 43.1 | 35.5 | 26.5 | 12.6 | | | | | | |
| Dursley | 101.4 | 91.8 | 81.3 | 72.5 | 63.5 | 54.6 | 47.0 | 38.1 | 24.1 | 11.6 | | | | | |
| Wotton under Edge | 113.2 | 103.6 | 93.1 | 84.3 | 75.3 | 66.4 | 58.8 | 49.8 | 35.9 | 23.3 | 11.8 | | | | |
| Hawkesbury | 125.0 | 115.5 | 104.9 | 96.2 | 87.1 | 78.2 | 70.7 | 61.7 | 47.8 | 35.2 | 23.6 | 11.9 | | | |
| Tormarton | 137.4 | 127.9 | 117.3 | 108.6 | 99.5 | 90.6 | 83.1 | 74.1 | 60.2 | 47.6 | 36.0 | 24.3 | 12.4 | | |
| Cold Ashton | 148.1 | 138.5 | 128.0 | 119.2 | 110.1 | 101.2 | 93.7 | 84.7 | 70.8 | 58.2 | 46.6 | 34.9 | 23.0 | 10.6 | |
| Bath | 164.5 | 154.9 | 144.4 | 135.7 | 126.6 | 117.7 | 110.2 | 101.2 | 87.2 | 74.7 | 63.1 | 51.4 | 39.5 | 27.1 | 16.5 |

# Notes